SERENITY HERE AND NOW

"The mindful
Who have attained Serenity
In this very birth
Are always tranquil
And they in this world
Have transcended desire."

—The Buddha Hemakamanavapuccha, 4

By the Same Author

Religion and Philosophy

Major Religions of India
Divine Messengers of Our Time
Homage to Yogaswami
The Pure in Heart
Miraculous Waters of Lourdes
Servant of God: Sayings of a Self-Realised Sage Swami Ramdas
My Philosophy of Life

Buddhism

New Insights into Buddhism
Nirvana the Highest Happiness
The First and Best Buddhist Teachings
Serenity Here and Now

J. Krishnamurti

J. Krishnamurti As I Knew Him
Living and Dying From Moment to Moment
That Pathless Land
Bliss of Reality
Sayings of J. Krishnamurti
A Bibliography of the Life and Teachings of Jiddu Krishnamurti
Jiddu Krishnamurti: A Bibliographical Guide

Library Science

Staff Exchanges in Librarianship
In-Service Training in Librarianship
The Role of Conferences in the Further Education of Librarians

Drama

The Pleasures of Life

Short Stories

The Holy Guru and Other Stories
The Stranger & Other Stories
Mysterious Stories of Sri Lanka
The Homeless Life and Other Stories

Autobiographical Writings

So You Want to Emigrate to England, Mohandas
Memoirs of an Oriental Philosopher

Serenity Here and Now

The Buddha's Sutta-Nipata Sermons

SUSUNAGA WEERAPERUMA

New Age Books

ISBN: 978-81-7822-333-9

First Edition: Delhi, 2009

Published by

NEW AGE BOOKS

A-44 Naraina Industrial Area Phase-I

New Delhi 110028 (India)

Email: nab@vsnl.in

Website: www.newagebooksindia.com

Printed in India

at Shri Jainendra Press

A-45 Naraina Phase-I, New Delhi-110028

Acknowledgements

The only person who helped me to write this book was my wife Dr Claudia Weeraperuma, who not only revised and edited all my writings but also carried out some research into the meanings of ambiguous Pali and Sanskrit words. Thereafter Claudia embellished the book with black-and-white illustrations, and also made it computer-ready.

In the course of preparing this new translation of the *Sutta-Nipata* in a comprehensible modern idiom, I frequently consulted several useful books that are all mentioned in my Bibliography.

I cannot help feeling indebted to the following translators: Sir Robert Chalmers, V. Fausboll, E. M. Hare, John D. Ireland, N. A. Jayawickrama and K. R. Norman.

I am thankful for Thanissaro Bhikkhu's *Sutta-Nipata* translations that are posted on the Internet.

Contents

List of the Suttas

Preface

There is a general consensus among Buddhists that the *Sutta-Nipata* is probably the most ancient Buddhist scripture. "There is no older book in Buddhist literature than the *Sutta-Nipata*, and no earlier corpus of primitive Buddhist doctrine than it contains," wrote Sir Robert Chalmers in his *Buddha's Teachings, being the Sutta-Nipata or Discourse Collection* (1932). Interestingly, Lord Chalmers, the eminent Pali scholar, was once the Governor of Ceylon in British colonial times.

Serenity Here and Now consists of the final 47 suttas of the *Sutta-Nipata* along with my commentaries on some of them.

This new book is in fact a continuation of the preceding one called *The First and Best Buddhist Teachings : Sutta-Nipata Selections and Inspired Essays* (New Age Books, 2006) wherein its second half was solely devoted to discourses from the *Sutta-Nipata*.

I feel duty-bound to bring to the readers' attention that *The First and Best Buddhist Teachings* was in turn a continuation of *Nirvana the Highest Happiness: Meditations on Buddhist Issues* (New Age Books, 2006), which contained a few suttas from the *Sutta-Nipata*.

Therefore all the above-mentioned works are actually a trilogy on the *Sutta-Nipata*, although the two books before *Serenity Here and Now* also included writings that I have described as inspired essays on various aspects of Buddhism.

By reading these scriptures one can catch a glimpse of some of the prevailing social customs, practices and beliefs at the time of the Buddha. That India is long past, although then, as now, the land was riven by bitter religious controversies. The Buddha lived during the sixth century before Christ. In India it was an epoch of highly developed values and moral standards. A great many were preoccupied with the eternal verities of life. This fact is evident from the subtle and involved questions that people put to the Enlightened One.

The Buddha was usually treated with deference because of the general recognition that anyone who had managed to reach the very summit of spirituality was worthy of respect. Laypersons and ascetics were given to visiting the Buddha whenever it became known that he was in residence at a monastery. Even the proud and powerful ruling kings of that time paid homage to him, which indicated their realisation that the sacred was somehow superior to the secular. The world of the Buddha, despite its many imperfections, stands out in contrast to our present world that is characterised by insatiable greed and materialism.

Over the centuries various philosophers and erudite pundits have laboriously speculated about the essence and nature of Nirvana. They did use a lot of words when they tried in vain to describe the Indescribable. But the Buddha, as he had actually attained that exalted state, used only an absolute minimum of words when he alluded to the Absolute:

"*This incomparable island*
Wherein there is neither
Decay nor death,
Which I name as Nirvana,
Is no other than
Owning nothing
And wanting nothing"

(excerpted from the chapter The Incomparable Island)

One of the hallmarks of Illumination is "owning nothing and wanting nothing". Such aphoristic sayings abound in the *Sutta-Nipata*.

The total purification of oneself is indispensable for Enlightenment. Not surprisingly, the importance of inner cleansing is a recurrent theme in the *Sutta-Nipata*. There are the taints or the defilements of the mind that must be cleansed away. Purification also entails the elimination from the mind of all thoughts and images. Then one discovers a certain emptiness. The state of emptiness defies description. For the want of a better word we can call it nothingness.

At present, alas, our minds are thoroughly conditioned by innumerable factors. The conditioned mind habitually distorts perception, for it cannot help looking at things from a predetermined perspective or viewpoint. Only the mind that is totally devoid of viewpoints is capable of seeing with undistorted clarity. Such a mind has no philosophical, intellectual or ideological viewpoint whatsoever. Several suttas have dealt with this subject. The translations of these suttas can be found in the following chapters: *Dropping All Philosophical Views*, *Can Philosophy Purify Us? The Wisdom of Having No Views*, *Desist from Debates*, *What Makes Us Quarrel? There is Only One Truth* and *Munis Eschew Every View.*

In the chapter *Be Mindful Always* the Buddha thus advised Mogharaja:

"*By looking at*
The emptiness
Or the void
That characterises the world,
And by dropping the view that
The 'self' exists,
One defeats death."

The view that Buddhism is a very cerebral religion is fairly widespread in the modern world. But the realisation that abandoning the machinery of the mind preludes nothingness might come as a complete surprise to those who have the mistaken impression that Buddhism is comprehensible only to the very intellectual.

No religious writer should arrogate to himself the right to write with the authoritative air of papal infallibility. By the same token, no translator, unless he has himself attained the exalted state of an Arhat, can claim to have a perfect understanding of the Dharma. The writer of this book, along with countless other visible and invisible beings, is still a fellow sufferer in the stormy sea of Samsara. Therefore there is an inevitable element of subjectivity in all my interpretations. In addition, every statement in this work is open to criticism and correction. I take the blame for any error or misunderstanding on my part.

In what ways do my methods and approach to the subject differ from those of the mainstream translators of yesteryear?

First, I do not regard writing or translating as purely intellectual pursuits. For when I use the intellect for these purposes, my thinking, as is usually the case, is harmoniously blended with devotion (*Bhatti*) and faith (*Saddha*). I believe that one can have a good grasp of the Dharma by using the head in conjunction with the heart. It is significant that the *Sutta-Nipata* ended on a devotional note. For the holy ascetic Pingiya had the good fortune to hear the following final words of the Buddha:

"Just as Vakkali,
Who was given to faith
And found release,
And Bhadravudha
Along with Alavi-Gotama,
In the same way
May you be freed

Through faith
And may you, Pingiya,
Proceed beyond
The realm of death."

Second, I have avoided falling into the trap of thinking that these ancient scriptures should be interpreted in a way acceptable to the Western Christian-orientated psyche. The pioneering translators were certainly dedicated to their work, but they had a liking for archaic forms of expression. Their practice of using words and phrases of bygone centuries confused many a modern reader. Probably they believed that certain honorific titles and sacred sayings were best indicated in a biblical style. I have, for instance, translated the term "Bhagava" as "Venerable", whereas some early translators with their theistic backgrounds preferred the term "Blessed One" as though the Divine or some other external agency had given the Buddha the blessing of Nirvana. I have always felt uneasy whenever I came across the term "Blessed One", which raised several important questions. Was Nirvana a favour or a generous gift from God? Was the Buddha a blessed Son of God? Not by the wildest stretch of imagination could anyone conceive of the Buddha in theistic terms. Such theism is contrary to both the letter and the spirit of Gotama's teachings with its strong emphasis on attaining Enlightenment by means of absolute self-reliance. That man is his own saviour is a distinguishing and basic Buddhist principle.

In this book, as in all my previous writings on the Dharma, I have tried my best to render the ancient scriptures in a contemporary idiom, remembering how old-fashioned language had put newcomers off Buddhism.

Third, since I am not a poet, I am not able to render the Pali stanzas into rhyming English poetry. But I am not sure if that could be done to perfection in any language. Fortunately, I have not tried to do that impossible task. However, in this translation the statements of the Buddha are in free verse.

Fourth, in the text the Buddha's words are always given in *italics*, which device enables the readers to differentiate easily the words of the Master from those of others, such as commentators, disciples, interviewers and the like.

Fifth, the substance of a translation, needless to say, is far more important than the form in which it has been made known. The traditional translators did serve the world up to a point with their meticulously accurate word-for-word translations. Although they were faithful to the original Pali texts, on the whole they succeeded in producing purely literal translations. Because of their rather academic approach to their work their translations tended towards unintelligibility. Those interested in the teachings were therefore beset with the practical problem of deciphering and digesting the Dharma. The Dharma, deep and difficult as it is, was now made doubly difficult to understand because many translators failed to explain the underlying meanings of certain obscure or unclear statements in the texts. The esoteric meanings are often the hidden treasures that should be unearthed for the benefit of mankind. Consequently, while remaining faithful to the original texts, I tried to capture the meaning of whatever was covert and then explain it.

In conclusion, I wish to write about the personal reasons for writing not only *Serenity Here and Now* but also the entire trilogy. Why have I written at length about the great truths that are discoverable in the Dharma?

My lifelong interest in the personality and teachings of Gotama the Buddha is my sole raison d'être. Luckily, I was born and raised in Sri Lanka where the Buddha Dharma, it is said, is still preserved in its pristine purity. Naturally, I am familiar with time-honoured Buddhist practices, such as observing the eight precepts on full moon days, offering food and medicines to monks, giving generously to the needy, feeding animals and never injuring or killing them, listening to the all-night sonorous chants of monks, going on pilgrimages to faraway ancient temples and enjoying the sight of colourful street processions that included drummers, Kandyan dancers and majestically caparisoned elephants. The central tenets of the Dharma were also as well known to me as the very tall and gracefully swaying coconut palms that line the sandy sea shores of Sri Lanka.

Great is the joy of exploring the Dharma and discussing it with likeminded seekers of the Truth. I write more in the spirit of a serious student with an enquiring mind than in that of an erudite professor with dogmatic and settled views. So if in the course of studying the suttas I discover something of significance that is seemingly new, it makes me feel happy. Whenever I have had a new insight into the Dharma, I almost instinctively like to share it with friends and readers who are scattered all over the globe. Although my inward quest is essentially a private one, I like to be of some assistance to other devotees by drawing their attention to helpful instructions in the texts that have unfortunately remained unnoticed.

Over the years several Buddhists informed me that the Enlightened One's discourses in the *Sutta-Nipata* had been to them exactly like the cleansing waters of the deep. With those fresh waters they had managed to purify their minds and hearts.

I must mention the name of Dr E. W. Adikaram in this connection. He was an eminent Pali scholar, author, educationist and historian whose magnum opus was titled *Early History of Buddhism in Ceylon.* Dr Adikaram, a very close friend of mine, once told me as follows:

"I derive all my religious sustenance from the *Sutta-Nipata.* It is the *only* Buddhist book I keep in my study! More than in any other Buddhist scripture, this book contains the essence of what the Tathagata taught."

During his lifetime this famous Sri Lankan recluse was nicknamed "*Sutta-Nipata* Buddhist" on account of his declared partiality for the *Sutta-Nipata.*

Vast and ocean-like are the Buddhist scriptures. Given the overwhelming immensity of Buddhist literature in various languages, including the texts of the different schools of thought, one wonders whether or not it is feasible to read them all, taking into consideration the very limited lifespan of a normal human being. Even if an energetic scholar or an ardent Buddhist succeeds in reading and studying everything, can he for that reason ever be sure that he has correctly understood all the subtleties of the Dharma? Out of the realisation that the mastery of this huge literature was well nigh impossible, I decided to confine my studies to the *Sutta-Nipata.*

It was the sheer profundity of the *Sutta-Nipata* that moved me to translate it into contemporary English. May the contents of this sacred book be a rich source of inspiration for all spiritual aspirants!

Susunaga Weeraperuma

1

Codes of Conduct for Renunciants and Laypersons

A certain saintly devotee called Dhammika, along with five hundred other lay devotees, approached the Buddha one day when the latter was living at Savatthi in Jeta's Grove. These devotees were all anagamins or never-returners as they had fully overcome the two obstacles — sense desires and ill-will.

Neither is an anagamin reborn in this world nor in a celestial one as he has eliminated every trace of sensuality. After his life has ended he is reborn in the Pure Abodes (*Suddhavasa*) where he attains the exalted state of Arhatship and is never again reborn.

These laypersons had taken the Uposatha vows, which are described below, on the day in question. They sought the Buddha's advice, as they were keen on knowing the difference between the life of a renunciant and that of a layperson.

After greeting the Master, Dhammika sat on one side of him and started speaking in stanzas. Now we can carefully look at the contents of the *Dhammikasutta* that are as follows:

1. *Dhammika: "O Gotama of immense intelligence,*
   Does one become a good disciple

By leaving the home to lead the homeless life,
Or by remaining a lay-follower?"

2. *"You are well aware of the ways of the worlds*
Of gods and men,
And the final goal.
None knows the subtle goal as well as you do.
They rightly call you
The Awakened One."

3. *"Out of compassion for living beings*
You have set forth the Dharma.
Casting aside the veil of darkness,
You have clarity of vision.
Free from blemish,
You fill the world with light.

4. *"After hearing that you were the Conqueror (Jina),*
Eravana the king of elephants consulted with you.
He was enchanted.
'Very good!' he remarked while going away."

5. *"King Vessavana Kuvera, too, posed questions*
Relating to the Dharma.
You, O wise Sage,
Answered when questioned.
After hearing you speak, he also was delighted."

6. *"Men who are standing*
Do not overtake the one
Who is walking swiftly.
The heretical teachers —
The Ajivikas and the Niganthas —
They don't surpass you in intelligence."

7. *"All these contentious Brahmins,*
And even some elderly Brahmins, including other debaters,
Are all bound by your Truth."

8. *"This profound and pleasant Dharma*

That has been so well expounded
By you, O holy one,
Which we are longing to hear,
O best of the Buddhas,
Explain it to us when we ask."

9. *"Let all the monks and laypersons who are seated here*
Listen and learn the Teachings
From the stainless Sage,
Just as the celestial beings listen
To the good words of Indra (Vasava)."

Monks

10. *The Buddha: "Hear me, O monks,*
I will instruct you in the Dharma
That destroys the defilements;
And do remember it, all of you.
Let the wise man who is thoughtful
And keen on the goal
Adopt the lifestyle of the religious renunciant."

11. *"A monk must not beg for alms at an untimely hour.*
Only at the prescribed time
Should he go to the village for this purpose.
Those who go at the wrong time
Become trapped in ties.
Therefore the Buddhas
Avoid making their alms rounds during improper periods."

12. *"Without becoming intoxicated*
By forms, sounds, tastes, smells and touch,
Let him at the correct time
Enter the village for the morning meal."

13. *"After having received his food at the right time,*
And after having returned alone,
He sits separately in solitude.

Then with watchful intelligence
He collects his thoughts
And turns his mind in an inward direction,
Away from outward distractions."

14. *"In case he should speak with a disciple,*
Or with someone else, or with a monk,
Let him talk about the exalted Dharma,
Without making slanderous statements
Nor blaming anyone."

15. *"For some argue and fight back when they are blamed;*
We cannot praise those who are lacking in good judgement.
They are attached to this or that
With their faraway minds."

16. *"Let the disciple of the one with wonderful wisdom,*
Having heard the Dharma from his Lord,
Seek alms-food, lodging
And water for washing the dirt from his upper robe."

17. *"Like an unclinging waterdrop*
That rests on a lotus leaf,
Let the monk never cling to his alms-food, lodging
Nor water for washing the dirt from his upper robe."

Laypersons

18. *"Now, on the other hand,*
I shall talk about the life of a layperson
And the means whereby he becomes a good disciple.
For the obligations of a monk
Cannot be fully fulfilled by one
Who is burdened with possessions."

19. *"After having eschewed violence*
Against all beings,
Both the strong and the trembling,
Let him neither kill

Nor cause any creature to be killed.
Let him not sanction
The destruction of life by others."

20. *"Let the disciple*
Never take anything from any place,
Being aware
That it has not been specifically given to him
And that it belongs to another.
Let him not incite theft
Nor approve it.
Let him avoid stealing."

21. *"The wise steer clear*
Of a burning charcoal pit.
Likewise, let the disciple
Avoid leading an unchaste life.
If he is not able to lead a pure life,
At least he should not seduce another's wife."

22. *"Let him not tell a falsehood*
Either in an assembly hall
Or alone to an individual;
Let him not cause others to tell lies
Nor approve of them that do so.
Let him avoid telling anything
That is not truthful."

23. *"Realising that the consumption of intoxicants*
Results in madness,
Let the layperson who agrees with this Dharma
Avoid taking intoxicants;
And let him not cause others to take them,
Nor approve of those
Who are given to drinking."

24. *"Out of intoxication*
The foolish not only do misdeeds

But also induce others to take intoxicants.
One should refrain from this misdeed,
This insanity,
This folly,
This delight of the stupid."

Uposatha (*Eightfold Observance*)

25. *"Let him not kill any living creature;*
Let him not take what has not been given him;
Let him not tell falsehoods;
Let him not take intoxicating drinks;
Let him avoid sexual impurity;
Let him not at night have ill-timed meals."

26. *"Let him not wear garlands nor use perfumes.*
Let him rest on a couch or mat
That is spread on the earth.

This they term the Uposatha,
The eightfold observance,
Which the Buddha explained,
Who transcended suffering."

27. *"Next, with devotion*
Do the observances,
Consisting of the Eight Precepts,
On the prescribed days of the month."

28. *"After performing his observances,*
Let the man of understanding and piety,
According to his means,
Offer food and drink to the monks in the morning."

29. *"Let him by the Dharma*
Maintain his mother and father.
In accordance with the Dharma
Let him earn his living righteously.

The vigilant disciple who lives in this manner
Is reborn among the celestial beings
Called Sayampabha ('self-luminant')."

This discourse is noteworthy as the Buddha insists on the strict adherence to the Five Precepts (*Pancha Sila*). These precepts are the foundation of all personal and social morality. These practices also help to ensure a certain well-ordered society, at least superficially: real orderliness springs only from inner purification, which is the fruit of meditation.

In many Buddhist societies it is often the case that public meetings begin with the communal recitation in Pali of the Five Precepts. Many pretend to be genuine Buddhists for frequently their recitations are only mere displays of piety. People, alas, make a great show of the recitation of the Precepts in public. Only the serious and the sincere realise the supreme importance of actually observing the Precepts in thought, word and deed not only in public but also in private.

2

Moving Forwards

The **Pabbajjasutta**, which is a discourse on the Going-forth, is particularly interesting and valuable because this sutta gives its seal of approval, as it were, to the ascetic way of living.

The word "Pabbajja" conjures up several thoughts in the mind relating to real renunciation. "Pabbajja" means giving up all one's mundane attachments in every sense of the word. That detachment from the world finds full expression in the act of becoming a monk or a nun. It is the Going-forth into the insecure homeless state, after casting aside the security and the comforts of hearth and home. Strictly speaking, it is the severing of all family ties and all emotional and other links with people and things, including the cessation of every craving for power, position and prestige. Does any abandoning of the world actually take place if a monk or nun "leaves society" with the hidden ambition of becoming a distinguished or a famous hermit? So subtle indeed are the tricks of the "I" that it is often hell-bent on asserting itself in a thousand different ways.

Their saffron-coloured robes do confer an elevated social status on renunciants. They thus acquire a certain reverential respectability. They then tend to become swollen-headed with the result that they start using their robes as a cover for their conceit or pride (*Mana*), which is one of the 10 fetters that indicate their enslavement to existence. Is there any guarantee that the "I" will die merely by wearing a coloured robe and leading a solitary life? That hardly happens. But constant vigilance or acute awareness of the hidden forces that operate within the mind will wash away pride. The mind of its own accord is then suddenly peaceful and alert.

Thus spoke Ananda:

1. *I will sing the praises of the Going-forth,*
   Such as the Going-forth of the Seer,
   Who with vision examined it
   And took delight in leading the ascetic life.
2. *Understanding that the household life*
   Is a limitation and a region of impurity,
   He chose homelessness
   In preference to homelife.
3. *As an ascetic,*
   By refraining from bad bodily behaviour
   And by avoiding the use of wrongful words,
   He led a good clean life.
4. *The Buddha went to Rajagaha,*
   And with all the splendid signs of a great being
   He entered the Giribbaja gorge of Magadha
   For the purpose of receiving alms.
5. *King Bimbisara,*
   While standing in his palace
   And seeing these signs of a supreme sage,
   Started speaking.
6. *King Bimbisara:*
   "Listen to him, Sirs,
   For this man is beautiful, great, pure

And a person of moral character,
Who looks not beyond the length of a plough."

7. *'With eyes cast in a downward direction,*
He is quite unlike the lowborn.
Let the royal messengers run and ask the monk:
'Where are you going?'"

8. *As the royal messengers followed him,*
They started wondering
'Where will the monk go?
Where will he be staying?'

9. *Keeping a watchful eye on his sense-doors,*
With an alert mind
He moved from door to door while begging for alms.
Before long the begging bowl became full.

10. *After going in search of alms-food,*
The Sage left the city
And went to the Pandava mountain
To find a dwelling place.

11. *Noticing that he had found a place to stay,*
The messengers then sat down.
But one returning messenger
Reported the matter to the King.

12. *Messenger: 'That monk, O great king,*
Is sitting on the Eastern side of the Pandava Mountain.
He is like a tiger or a bull;
He is like a lion inside his cave."

13. *Upon hearing these words,*
The Kshatriya or warrior-king
Rushed to the Pandava Mountain
In a beautiful chariot.

14. *After travelling*
As far as the ground was suitable for his chariot,

The king next stepped out of his vehicle,
And went towards him on foot.
The king sat beside him.

15. *The king, who was sitting, exchanged greetings.*
After such pleasant conversation,
The king exclaimed in delight:

16. *King Bimbisara:*
"You are both young and tender,
A lad in the first flush of youth
With a fair complexion and fine form,
Like a high-born Kshatriya

17. *Who adorns the vanguard of the army,*
At the head of the chiefs.
I will give you riches. Do enjoy them!
But do disclose your lineage,
When requested to do so."

18. *The Buddha: "Just next to the Himalayas, O king,*
There lives a people who have both riches and energy —
The Kosalans."

19. *"By lineage we are of the Adiccas —*
'The solar race',
And by birth we are Sakyans.
From that family I have Gone-forth,
Not craving for sensuous pleasures."

20. *"Seeing that the pursuit of sensuous pleasures*
Is attended with peril,
And having found peace and relaxation
In renunciation —
The Going-forth,
I delight in doing just this."

3

The Struggle of the Sakyan Sage

Prince Siddhartha, the Bodhisattva or the Buddha-to-be, suddenly abandoned his palace at the age of 29, choosing not to succeed to his father's throne but instead to ponder over mankind's inner malaise. In the eyes of his contemporaries, the prince's refusal to take on the conventional role of father to his newborn babe must have seemed like the rash decision of an irresponsible young man. But deep was his conviction that all his time and energy ought to be devoted to better things.

What really happened during the 6 long years following the great Renunciation? The traditionally accepted view is that he spent his time destroying his defilements by a rigorous and very austere process of suppression. We are told that he wrestled with his psychological tendencies or traits and managed to get rid of them once and for all.

There is a divergent view about the Bodhisattva, which is not widely accepted, but is nevertheless worthy of consideration. There are some who seriously maintain that the Bodhisattva's personality traits or defilements, which had kept him in servitude for countless births, just dropped to their death of their own accord. This took place without a struggle, but only after he

…stood the hidden nature of his defilements. … other words, was the fruit of intense self- … meditative watchfulness. He came by this Illumination. It dawned on him by chance in the sense that it did not originate in anything. Now one can see why it is said that Nirvana is without cause. It was not one of those cheap and chemically induced short-lived "states of altered consciousness". It was *outside* the field of karma. Yet at the same time it must be admitted that this happy happening was the outcome of years of inner investigation and purification. We have chosen to call this process "struggle" for want of a more accurate expression, despite the fact that "struggle" seems something of a misnomer.

Let us examine the text of the **Padhanasutta** or the discourse on striving or struggling:

1. *The Buddha: "While I, being so keen on striving,*
   Was meditating near the Neranjara River
   For the finding of Nirvanic security,
2. *Namuci (a name of Mara) approached me*
   And spoke sympathetically,"
   Mara: "You are very thin,
   Not pleasant in appearance
   And on the verge of death."
3. *"Whereas a thousand parts of you*
   Are owned by death,
   Only one part of you
   Is owned by life.
   Venerable One,
   It is better to live your life.
   By living you can do meritorious deeds."
4. *"By leading a holy life*
   And by feeding the sacrificial fire

You will acquire much merit.
But by striving what will you achieve?"

5. *"The path of striving is difficult to tread.*
It is difficult to do
And difficult to succeed,"
Said Mara, who was standing next to the Buddha.

6. *To Mara's words the Master said in reply,*
The Buddha: "O Evil One,
Friend of the lazy,
Why have you come here?"

7. *"I do not need even one jot of merit.*
Mara should speak to those
Who have that need."

8. *"Within me can be found*
Faith, energy and wisdom.
Why do you ask me to live
When I am keen on striving?"

9. *"This wind is drying up*
Even the currents of rivers.
Will it not gradually dry up
My blood
In the course of striving?"

10. *"When my mind is dried up*
And the bile and the phlegm are all withered,
And when the flesh is decayed,
My mind becomes serene.
Then there is more mindfulness
And greater insight."

11. *"While living in this manner,*
Having experienced
Painful sensations,
My mind is not in search

Of sensual pleasures.
Mara, see the state of purity!"

12. *"Sensuality is your first army;*
Your second is discontent;
Your third is hunger and thirst
And your fourth is craving."

13. *"Your fifth army is sloth and torpor;*
Your sixth is timidity;
Your seventh is doubt or uncertainty,
And your eighth is hypocrisy and stupor."

14. *"Your ninth army is gain and honour,*
And falsely received renown;
And your tenth is the overestimation of yourself
And the underestimation of others."

15. *"Such, Namuci (a name of Mara), is your fighting force.*
None but a hero manages to defeat it.
Having subdued it,
The conqueror is blissfully happy."

16. *"See, I wear munja grass!*
I don't care at all about life here!
Dying in the battlefield
Is better than living a defeated life."

Soldiers decorated their weapons and themselves with strings of munja grass around their heads, thus symbolising that there can be no turning back.

17. *"Some ascetics and Brahmins*
Have become entangled in this world.
They do not stand out.
They do not know the path trodden
By the virtuous."

18. *"Seeing the soldiers who are all in battle array,*
With Mara riding on his elephant,

I will go out to fight him.
May he not oust me from my place!"

19. *"This army of yours,*
Which neither gods nor men can crush to death,
I will crush it
With wisdom,
As with a stone
One would smash an unfired earthen pot."

20. *"Having power over my thoughts*
And with well-established mindfulness,
I will go about from realm to realm,
And instruct a great many disciples."

21. *"They, being alert*
And awake
As well as earnest,
Will practise the teachings
Of the one who is lust-free.
They will do so despite your opposition.
They will go there,
And having gone there,
They will not regret it."

22. *Mara: "For a period of seven years*
I did follow the Holy One step by step,
But I failed to find any fault
In the Supremely Awakened One,
Who has mindfulness."

23. *"A crow moved round and round a stone,*
Which bore a resemblance to a lump of fat,
Mistakenly believing that
'Perhaps it is soft' or 'perhaps it is sweet'."

24. *"Disappointed,*
Failing to find anything sweet,
The crow flew away.

Likewise, disappointed in Gotama,
We shall leave him."

25. *The Buddha: "Utterly grief-stricken,*
His lute slipped from his armpit
And fell down.
The dejected spirit disappeared
Then and there."

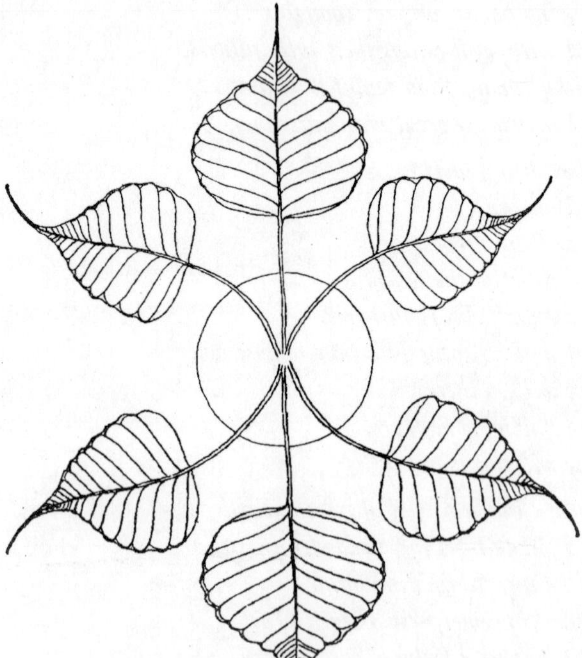

4

What are Well – Spoken Words ?

The Buddha, who was in residence in the Jeta Grove at Savatthi, gave one of his many addresses to the monks. The **Subhasitasutta** is the report of his discourse on using well-chosen words when talking. One can reasonably assume that the practice of using well-chosen words extends also to writing and all other forms of verbal communication.

The Buddha: "Only in four respects, O monks,
Can one regard words as being well-spoken,
Not badly-spoken,
Which are faultless and blameless
To those with great understanding.
What are these four?
O monks, a monk is well-spoken,
Not badly-spoken;
He only speaks what is righteous,
Not what is unrighteous;
He only speaks what is pleasant,
Not what is unpleasant;
He only speaks what is true,
Not what is false."

This is what the Master said.

Sugato or the Happy Farer — Sugato is an epithet of a Buddha — then proceeded to explain as follows:

1. *"What is well-spoken, the virtuous rank first;*
One must speak what is righteous,
Not what is unrighteous,
This ranks second;
One must speak what is pleasant,
Not what is unpleasant,
This ranks third;
And one must speak what is true,
Not what is false,
This ranks fourth."

The Venerable Vangisa rose from his seat, adjusted his robe by placing it on one shoulder and saluted the Master with hands clasped together.

Vangisa: "O Sugato, it occurs to me — "

The Buddha: "*What is it that occurs to you, Vangisa?*"

Thereupon Vangisa rose to his feet and was full of praise for the Buddha. Vangisa expressed himself in verse:

2. *"One must only use words*
That neither hurt others
Nor oneself.
Such words are well-spoken ones indeed."

3. *"One should, when speaking,*
Only use pleasant words that others welcome.
Pleasant are the words that convey
No evil to other persons."

4. *"Truth is immortal speech:*
This is an eternal verity.
They say the virtuous are grounded

In what is true,
Good and right."

5. *"The words of the Buddha, which he spoke*
For the attaining of Nirvana
And the ending of suffering,
Far surpass all other spoken words."

In the light of the above-mentioned criteria, we can consider the following fairly typical everyday situations where people are involved.

The scene is a consulting room.

"Haven't I told you many times that you have to lose weight soon?" shouts the doctor at an obese lady. "Unless you do so," he continues, "you will become a candidate for a terrible heart attack. Why not become slim instead of looking like an ugly fat pig?"

Although the doctor is well intentioned, he uses unpleasant words, because he believes that there is no other way of convincing his patient. It is a case of the doctor giving the right advice, but he couches it in hurtful language.

The next scene is an outdoor meeting during an election campaign.

The leader of a political party makes a speech: "Only our party can solve the unemployment problem, reduce taxation and ensure a period of uninterrupted peace and prosperity throughout the entire land. Crime will disappear altogether and the general level of prices will fall..."

At the hustings candidates are lavish with promises, only to break them once they get positions of power. Although we know only too well that many politicians are prone to promise the moon before any election, unfortunately it is the case that the vast majority of constituents simply allow themselves to be swayed by insincere talk. Politicians, by falsely assuring gullible people that their future is going to be rosy, when they do not really mean it in the least, cleverly win votes! Sweetly pleasant words they certainly use, but are they truthfully spoken?

A cunning man starts courting an innocent country lass.

"Yours is the most beautiful and charming face I've ever seen," he tells her untruthfully, trying his best to flatter her.

She foolishly believes the stranger, as she is not intensely observant and hence incapable of seeing through him. So when he promises to marry her, she readily agrees to the idea. Next he goes to bed with her, but soon afterwards he jilts her, and starts chasing a new woman he has just met.

The mindful, being always watchful of the ways of their egos, who are constantly aware of their vanity that craves to be fed with compliments, soon develop a natural immunity to flattery. They remain indifferent to praise. The mindful cannot be easily deceived.

I shall never forget the casual remark of an Iranian friend. "In my country," he proudly said, "it is considered sinful to tell a lie but in France lying has developed into a refined art!" He might not have known that in actual fact the practice of lying is fairly common right throughout the world. Such is our degeneration that lying is now more the norm than the exception even in so-called highly educated and civilised societies.

Why is it that some are not seized by pangs of conscience when making false statements? People lie for a thousand different reasons. Prisoners on trial, for instance, yield to the temptation to tell lies in order to prove their innocence. They like to distort facts with the intention of lessening the severity of the punishments for their crimes.

At interviews for jobs applicants tend to tell fibs because of their eagerness to make an impression. Little do they realise that lying is counter-productive. Once they are discovered lying, who will want to trust them? A saying ascribed to Abraham

Lincoln is that no man has so good a memory as to be a successful liar. The world might fail to notice or even completely forget our lies, but does the karmic law operate in that manner?

Compulsive liars utter falsehoods as they cannot help it: they are not able to control or change completely their complex condition. There are also people who like to lie for the sheer fun of it: they get a kick out of lying. They obtain a feeling of intense pleasure or excitement by fooling others. Simply seeing the discomfiture (embarrassment or confusion) of others provides these liars with a certain sadistic pleasure. Some like practical jokes, involving the telling of lies, just for the sake of amusement. What might outwardly look like a little bit of harmless fun might in fact spring from hidden hurts and lurking ill will.

Fiction writing involves the invention of stories. Are we going to discard literature merely because it consists of concoctions of interesting and entertaining accounts? What do we make of myths and moral fables that are part of our tradition and civilisation? Surely it would seem silly to frown upon such writings, especially when one of their principal purposes is the illustration of hidden principles or truths.

The fourth of the Five Precepts (*Panca Sila*) that every serious Buddhist observes, or at least tries to observe, is as follows:

Musavada veramani sikkha padam samadiyami

I take the precept to abstain from false speech.

Nowadays, alas, this precept is increasingly honoured more in the breach than in the observance. Both by precept and example, the elders and parents in Buddhist societies should try to inculcate in the young a sense of morality. If only the adults actually abstain from telling lies, including white lies, instead of always lecturing the young about it, that would surely be an effective and eloquent expression of the teachings relating to right speech. Not only the students but also the public at large are in need of a practical demonstration of the fact that whenever people become truthful, society also inevitably becomes orderly, harmonious and peaceful.

In *The Word of the Buddha* by the Venerable Nyanatiloka there is an excellent explanation of Samma-Vaca or Right Speech, which is the Third Step of the eight steps that constitute the Noble Eightfold Path.

What is Right Speech? Put briefly, one abstains from lying, tale-bearing, harsh language and vain talk.

Abstaining from Lying

One not only avoids lying but also speaks the truth in all situations and at all times. He never bears false witness against anyone. Whenever he is summoned to say what he knows, being a witness who is always devoted to the truth, he would answer either "I know nothing", or "I know", or "I have seen nothing" or "I have seen". Thus he never lies knowingly, either for his own advantage or for that of another.

Abstaining from Tale-Bearing

One must not be given to gossiping or tale-bearing in the sense that one should avoid repeating in one place what one has heard elsewhere. Thereby there will be an avoidance of discord. One avoids repeating the gossip that one hears. What should gladden us is not social discord but social concord: the latter we can promote by means of adhering to Right Speech.

Abstaining from Harsh Language

The one who refrains from harsh language would naturally prefer using words that are gentle, loving, soft, courteous, friendly and heart-warming. Words that are violent, crude, rude, obscene and disrespectful do not presumably fall into this category.

The Buddha: "You would not be regarded as my followers, O monks,

If you become angry,
Even if thieves and killers
Were to cut your limbs and joints with a saw.
Remain unruffled in mind
Without evil words escaping the lips.
Remain friendly and feel sympathy
With a love-filled heart.
Without any concealed ill will,
Permeate that person with a love
That is broad, profound, frontierless
And devoid of any anger and hate"

Majjhima Nikaya, no. 21

Abstaining from Vain Talk

One must eschew vain talk. One speaks only at the right time and what one says should be based on facts. Speak about what is useful, the law and the discipline. What is said should be sensible and sustained by arguments.

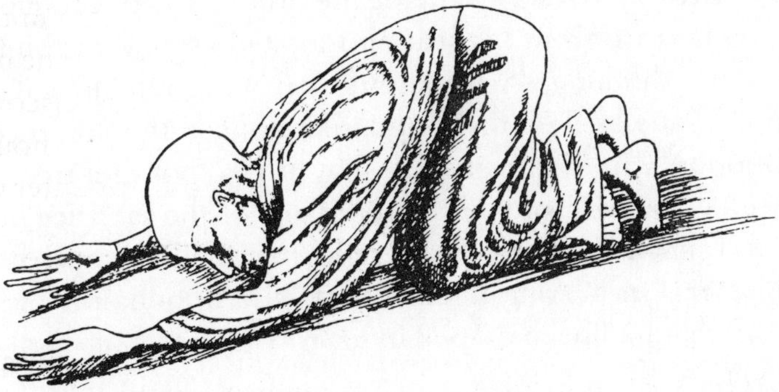

5

Who is Deserving of Offerings ?

A certain Brahmin, Sundarikabharadvaja by name, was in the process of making offerings to the sacrificial fire on the banks of the river Sundarika. As it happened, the Buddha was staying among the Kosala people on the banks of the very same river. This was the setting of the **Sundarika bharadvajasutta**.

Sundarika, in other words, was performing the Agnihotra sacrifice: milk, oil and sour gruel was offered to Agni, the god of fire. After Sundarika had made the offerings and worshipped the fire, he rose from his seat and looked around in the four directions, thinking, "who should eat what remains of this sacrifice?" It was then that Sundarika noticed the presence of the Buddha, who was seated closeby at the foot of a tree with his head covered. Holding the remnants of the sacrifice in his left hand and his water-pot in his right, the Brahmin approached the Master. On hearing his footsteps, the Buddha uncovered his head that had been draped in his robe.

"This shaven-headed man," thought Sundarika, "is just a shaveling", and so he wanted to turn back and go away. But it soon crossed his mind that "since some Brahmins here are shaven-headed I would like to go to this man and inquire about his ancestry". Thereupon Sundarika approached the Buddha and started speaking with him.

Sundarika: "What are you by birth?"

1. *The Buddha: "I am not a Brahmin for sure,*
Nor the son of a king;
Neither am I a merchant
Nor do I belong to any rank.
Well do I know the common worldlings.
Being unattached to the world,
I wander in the world
Without owning anything."

2. *"Clad in robes of cast-off rags,*
Shaven and homeless,
I calmly go from one place to another,
Being unsullied by contact with human beings.
O Brahmin,
You ask me an impertinent question
About my origins!"

3. *Sundarika: 'No, Sir, when Brahmins meet, they always ask, 'are you a Brahmin?''"*
The Buddha: "If you claim to be a Brahmin
And deny that I am one of them,
Then chant me the Savitri
Consisting of three lines and twenty-four syllables."
(This refers to that famous Rig Vedic chant (iii-62-10)
"So that it may illuminate our minds,
Let us meditate on Savitar —
The Holiest Light
Of the Divine Sun"
Tat savitur varenyam
Bhargo devasya dhimai
Dhiyo yo nah prachodayat)

4. Sundarika: "What inspired so many sages, human beings, warriors and Brahmins in this world to make lavish sacrificial offerings to the gods?"

   The Buddha: "When a perfect person
   Who has understanding,
   Being one who has broken
   The chain of Samsara,
   Receives an offering from anyone
   At the time of sacrifice,
   I say that it will be fruitful to the donor."

5. Sundarika: "Surely my sacrifice will be fruitful, for we have seen one like you, who is a person of understanding. Had I not seen you, someone else would have eaten the sacrificial cake."

6. *The Buddha: "Therefore, O Brahmin,*
   Since you have cared to visit me
   In search of something,
   You may ask for it.
   Perhaps here you might meet one
   Who is serene,
   Free from anger,
   Free from distress,
   Free from desire,
   One with great insight."

7. Sundarika: "I take delight in making offerings, O Gotama. Although I wish to make an offering, I fail to understand it. Please instruct me. When will a sacrifice bear fruit?"

   The Buddha: "In that case, O Brahmin,
   Lend me your ear.
   I will teach you the Dharma."

8. *"Inquire not about ancestry:*
   Inquire about conduct.

From wood fire is born.
Likewise, although of lowly birth,
A Muni (Sage) becomes firm and noble
With the restraint born of humility."

9. *"One who is Truth-tamed*
And temperate,
Who has attained to the highest knowledge
And leads the holy life —
To such a person
Let the Brahmin, being keen on good works,
Make offerings at the right time."

10. *"No longer seeking sensual pleasures,*
These homeless wanderers
Are thoroughly restrained
And straight as a shuttle —
To such persons
Let the Brahmin, being keen on good works,
Make offerings at the right time."

11. *"They are lust-free*
With well-composed organs of sense.
Like the moon
That has managed to escape from Rahu's *clutches,*
They attained Release *—*
To such persons
Let the Brahmin, being keen on good works,
Make offerings at the right time."

12. *"Free from attachments,*
They wander around the earth,
Mindful at all times
And having no sense of 'mine' —
To such persons
Let the Brahmin, being keen on good works,
Make offerings at the right time."

13. *"The Tathagata (the Perfect One),*
Having transcended sensual pleasures,
Wanders victoriously.
Having ended the cycle of births and deaths,
He is supremely happy
Like the calm and cool waters of a lake,
The Tathagata
Is worthy of the sacrificial cake."

14. *"The equal of former Buddhas,*
The Tathagata is withdrawn
From lesser persons.
Of infinite intelligence
Is the Perfect One,
Who in this world is without blemish
Here or elsewhere.
The Tathagata
Is worthy of the sacrificial cake."

15. *"Within him there is neither*
Deceit nor conceit.
He is free from lust
And selfishness,
And devoid of desire
And anger.
That Brahmin,
Who has managed to wash off
The filth of grief,
Such a Tathagata
Is worthy of the sacrificial cake."

16. *"He no longer takes refuge*
In the escapist resting-places of the mind.
Being greed-freed,
He does not cling to anything
Either in the world here

Or elsewhere,
The Tathagata
Is worthy of the sacrificial cake."

17. *'Tranquil and attentive,*
He has crossed
The flood waters of existence.
Deeply does he the Dharma understand.
His passions are all extinct.
This is his last existence.
The Tathagata
Is worthy of the sacrificial cake."

18. *'The Asavas (the corruptions) of existence*
And harsh speech
Are there no more.
The Knower is liberated
In every respect,
The Tathagata
Is worthy of the sacrificial cake."

19. *'Being detached,*
He no longer has any ties.
Not taking pride in anything
Though being among the proud,
And thoroughly understanding
Both the basis
And the extent of suffering,
The Tathagatha
Is worthy of the sacrificial cake."

20. *'Not desiring anything,*
He comes by the seclusion
That is Nirvana.
He sees through the heresies of others.
There is nothing in him
That will give rise to rebirth.

The Tathagatha
Is worthy of the sacrificial cake."

21. *"He understands all forms of phenomena.*
These he has penetrated
With his profound insight.
Having penetrated them,
They have perished for good.
Having abandoned all attachments,
He is emancipated
And calm.
The Tathagata
Is worthy of the sacrificial cake."

22. *"Being free from fetters*
And the cycle of births,
He has put away sensuality.
He is pure, perfect,
Spotless and flawless.
The Tathagata
Is worthy of the sacrificial cake."

23. *"Seeing that there is no such thing*
As 'self' within oneself,
He is attentive
And he leads an upright life.
Being free from desire,
Obstinacy and doubt,
The Tathagata
Is worthy of the sacrificial cake."

24. *"Without having any delusion whatsoever,*
He has insight into every mental state.
With his final body,
He has attained
Incomparable Buddhahood.
Such is the purity of that spirit.

The Tathagata
Is worthy of the sacrificial cake."

25. Sundarika: "In the past I have made sacrificial offerings. Let this offering of mine be a true one, since I have met such a person as yourself, who has attained the highest knowledge. With Brahma as my witness, may the Exalted *One accept from me this sacrificial cake."*

26. *The Buddha: "What is gained by reciting verses, O Brahmin,*
Is not fit or proper to be eaten.
This is not the manner of the clear-sighted.
The verse-chanted food —
The Buddhas reject it.
As long as the Dharma lasts,
This is the mode of life."

27. *"For such deeds are performed*
By merit-seeking doers of good works.
But with other food and drink
Do serve the Perfect One
Whose passions did cease,
And who is now at peace."

28. Sundarika: "Very good, O Venerable One, who then should partake of an offering from one like me? Having accepted your advice, whom shall I seek at the time of sacrifice?"

29. *The Buddha: "He whose anger has gone,*
Whose mind is serene,
Who is fully lust-free
And not given to idling away his time."

30. *"The remover of limitations,*
Who knows the chain of births and deaths,
The Muni (Buddha)
With the attributes of a sage,
When such a being comes to a sacrifice —"

31. *"Without frowning,*
Hold up your clasped hands
As a sign of respectful greeting,
Pay homage to him with food and drink.
Thus your sacrifice will succeed."

32. Sundarika: "The Enlightened One, Lord, is worthy of the sacrificial cake. He is an incomparable field of merit, the most suitable recipient of sacrifice in the whole world. What is offered to you, O Lord, will bring forth great fruit."

The Brahmin Sundarikabharadvaja took refuge in the Buddha, the Dharma and the Sangha. The Buddha granted his request to receive both the ordination and the higher ordination. Before long, living alone, he was diligently engaged in striving. He did what needed doing. Thereafter he became, so to speak, part of that great galaxy of Arhats.

6

Gift - Giving and Merit – Making

A Brahmin youth by the name of Magha went to meet the Buddha, who was staying on the Vulture's Peak Mountain called Gijjhakuta. This famous retreat of the Sage, which is near Rajagaha, is situated picturesquely with panoramic views of surrounding valleys and mountains. Magha greeted the Buddha, exchanged pleasantries and sat on a side. Their ensuing conversation is reported in the **Maghasutta**:

Magha: "O Gotama, I am a generous giver of gifts. After earning my wealth by rightful means, I part with it, giving it away to a single person, two persons, three, four, five, six, seven, eight, nine, ten, twenty, thirty, forty, fifty, one hundred or even more. Tell me, Gotama, by so giving do I acquire much merit?"

The Buddha: "Certainly, young man,
In so giving
From rightly gained riches
One does obtain a lot of merit."

1. Magha: "O kind Gotama, the yellow-robed homeless wanderer, I wish to pose a question: If a liberal householder, being keen on merit-making, wishes to give others food

and drink, to whom should the offerings be made so that it will have a purificatory effect on the donor?"

2. *The Buddha: "O Magha,*
He who makes sacrifices
For the purpose of acquiring merit,
Such as giving food and drink,
These efforts
Will be crowned with success,
Provided the offerings are given
To gift-worthy recipients."

3. *Magha: "Tell me of gift-worthy recipients, O Exalted One."*

4. *The Buddha: "Those who wander*
The face of the earth
Without craving for anything,
Having nothing,
Being perfect and calm —
To them let the Brahmin make an offering."

5. *"Those who have broken*
All bonds and fetters,
Who are tamed and fully released,
And are free
From suffering and desire —
To them let the Brahmin make an offering."

6. *"Those who have terminated*
All ties,
Who are tamed and totally liberated,
And are free
From suffering and desire —
To them let the Brahmin make an offering."

7. *"Those who, having given up*
Greed, anger and delusion,
Being taintless,

Lead the religious life —
To them let the Brahmin make an offering."

8. *"Those within whom there is*
Neither deceit nor conceit,
Who are not under the control
Of greed,
And free from desire
As well as the sense of 'mine' (egotism) —
To them let the Brahmin make an offering."

9. *"Those who*
Without being under the influence
Of craving,
Have managed to cross
The flood of existence
And are entirely devoid
Of egotism —
To them let the Brahmin make an offering."

10. *"Those who crave not*
For anything of this world
Or for states of becoming
Either in this life
Or in an afterlife —
To them let the Brahmin make an offering."

11. *"Those who roam around,*
Having given up
The pleasures of the senses,
Being thoroughly restrained
And straight-forward like a shuttle —
To them let the Brahmin make an offering."

12. *"They are free from passion*
With unruffled faculties of sense.
Like the moon
That is liberated from Rahu's grasp,

They are fully emancipated —
To them let the Brahmin make an offering."

13. *"Those who are serene,*
Passionless
And devoid of anger,
And for whom,
After the ending of the present life,
There will be no afterlife —
To them let the Brahmin make an offering."

14. *"Those who have cast away*
The chain of births and deaths
And have transcended all doubt —
To them let the Brahmin make an offering."

15. *"Those who move about in this world,*
Remaining islands unto themselves,
Having nothing
And being completely released
In every respect —
To them let the Brahmin make an offering."

16. *"Those who in this world*
Realise the truth as it really is —
'This is the final birth:
There is no further rebirth' —
To them let the Brahmin make an offering."

17. *"Those who have succeeded*
In finding the highest knowledge,
Who are fond of meditation
And are thoughtful,
Having attained Enlightenment
And being a refuge to many —
To them let the Brahmin make an offering."

18. Magha: "Certainly mine was not a foolish inquiry! The Exalted One has informed me of those who are worthy of

gifts, for you know it as it actually is, as surely as you know the Dharma."

19. "If a merit-seeking and generous householder were to give food and drink to others here in this world, tell me, O Exalted One, of the success of such a sacrifice."

20. *The Buddha: "Sacrifice,*
But while making sacrifices,
O Magha, have a mind
That is purified in every way.
Sacrifice
Is the end towards which
The donor's efforts are directed.
Taking one's stand on this,
One gives up anger."

21. *"In this way,*
When attachments and anger
Are no longer there,
And there is limitless love,
The ever-vigilant one
Radiates goodwill everywhere."

22. Magha: "Who is pure? Who is released? Who is imprisoned? Acting alone, how can one go to the Brahma world? Answer me, O Exalted One, as I am ignorant. The Exalted One is my witness that I see Brahma today as you are like Brahma! O Brilliant One, how can one be reborn in the Brahma world?"

23. *The Buddha: "A generous individual,*
I declare,
Is reborn in the Brahma world.
Such a person prospers
Because the recipients of the gifts
Are worthy of them.

The success obtained by giving alms
Increases threefold."

After this conversation, Magha was so impressed by the Master that he took refuge in the Buddha, the Dharma and the Sangha. "May the Venerable Gotama," Magha requested, "accept me as a lay disciple until the end of my days."

Two truths emerge from this interesting dialogue between the Buddha and Magha. First, perfect or fully liberated beings like the Buddha and the Arhats are deserving of sacrifices, gifts, and alms such as food and drink. Second, we know that any offerings to them will be very meritorious. Does the text of this sutta suggest that only liberated beings are worthy of gifts? One can surmise that gifts presented to non-liberated beings would generate a lesser amount of merit than those given to the fully enlightened.

Since genuine saints, let alone Buddhas and Arhats, hardly live in our midst nowadays, we can instead offer alms to monks, nuns and reclusive laypersons who are serious in their inner quest. In addition, one could and indeed should provide the basic necessities for the destitute, the homeless and the unemployed. There are other categories of deprived people — war refugees and the victims of natural disasters such as floods and earthquakes.

One can disseminate information and knowledge by distributing books free of charge, especially Dharma books, acting in accordance with the famous Buddhist maxim: the gift of the Dharma exceeds all other gifts.

We can help the needy in a thousand different ways, regardless of whether our good works result in merit or not. Unless we are very cautious, there is the dangerous possibility of our developing a craving (*Tanha*) for accumulating merit as though it were something to be hoarded for future use. For we are aware that good deeds are productive of favourable and profitable karmic results. *Punna* or merit is the term used for describing actions that are karmically wholesome (*Kusala*).

Moved purely by compassion (*Karuna*) for suffering humanity, acting only out of the sheer goodness of their hearts, so to speak, some share what little they have with the less fortunate. When they give they neither request nor expect anything in return. Compassion-based actions are unpolluted by the hidden longing for recognition and rewards. Selfless and altruistic men and women, whose genuine generosity springs solely from compassion, tend to treat with utter indifference the sweet fruits of their charitable deeds. They not even want a little recompense.

As far as Arhats are concerned, they are beyond merit and demerit. According to the *Sutta Nipata*, Arhats never cling to merit or demerit, in the same manner that the lovely lotus never clings to water.

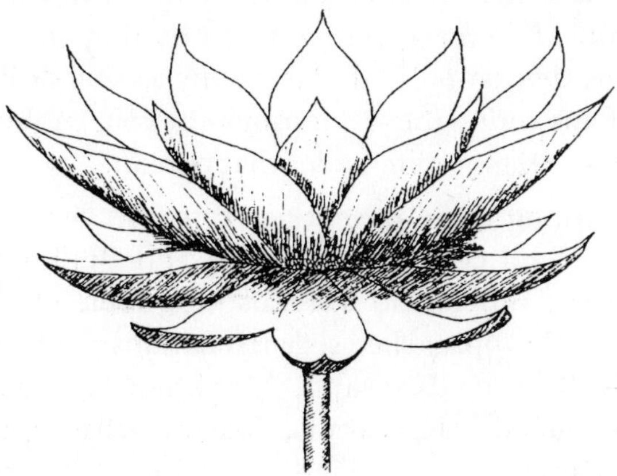

7

The Questions of a Wandering Ascetic

It is possible to get a great insight into the Buddha's teachings by focusing attention on the questions for which Sabhiya, the wandering ascetic, was trying to find answers. The **Sabhiyasutta** deals with these matters.

A deity, who in a previous existence on earth had been a blood relation of Sabhiya, put certain questions to Sabhiya. Thereafter the deity stipulated that "if any ascetic or Brahmin is capable of answering these questions for you, Sabhiya, then you must lead a religious life under that person."

After learning these questions from the deity, Sabhiya approached several celebrated recluses and Brahmins, who headed monastic orders and were also the founders of sects with followers. He approached six such famous teachers of his day, namely: Purana Kassapa, Makkhali Gosala, Ajita Kesakambali, Pakudha Kaccayana, Sanjaya Bellatthiputta and Nigantha Nataputta.

When Sabhiya posed his questions, none of the above-mentioned teachers was able to provide him with satisfactory answers. The situation was bad indeed. To make matters worse, these teachers, being incapable of giving the correct answers, not only reacted with anger but also retaliated by putting counter questions to the questioner. Poor Sabhiya suddenly thought, "what if I return to leading my degenerate life of former times and start indulging in sensual pleasures?"

Then it occurred to Sabhiya that he might ask Gotama. "This recluse Gotama," he thought, "is also the chief of a monastic order with disciples. Gotama is renowned and the founder of a religious group and he is highly esteemed by many. What if I go to Gotama and pose these questions?"

"Those venerable recluses and Brahmins whom I had previously visited," thought Sabhiya, "are aged and infirm, they are very experienced elders. They have long been homeless. They are leaders of orders with followers and they are also renowned and respected. They were annoyed when I questioned them. Besides, they talked back to me. Will Gotama be able to answer my questions, for he is young in years and a relative newcomer to asceticism?"

"No recluse," thought Sabhiya, "should be treated with indifference or dislike just because he is young. If he were young, he would have power and influence. I will visit Gotama and ask these questions."

The wandering ascetic continued with his journeys of pilgrimage and eventually arrived at Rajagaha and met the Buddha. The Squirrel's Sanctuary in the Bamboo Grove (*Veluvana*) at Rajagaha, where the squirrels were fed, was the quiet and idyllic setting for the *Sabhiyasutta*:

1. Sabhiya: "Wishing to ask questions, I come to you with anxiety and doubts. Do put an end to these doubts. When I pose questions, answer them in the regular order and explain in accordance with the Dharma."

2. *The Buddha: "Wishing to ask questions, O Sabhiya,*
   You have come from a faraway place.

I will put an end to those doubts.
I will answer your questions
In the regular order and explain
In accordance with the Dharma."

3. *"Ask me, O Sabhiya,*
Whatever question you have in mind.
I will put an end to each doubt."

"How wonderful! How marvellous!" thought Sabhiya, "for the ascetic Gotama has provided me with an opportunity that no other ascetic or Brahman has provided even to the smallest extent." Delighted, elated and extremely happy, Sabhiya posed a question:

4. *Sabhiya: "What should one accomplish to become a 'Bhikku'?*
When is one called 'humble' and 'tamed'?
Why is one called 'Enlightened'?
O Exalted One, explain this to me."

5. *The Buddha: "He, who by means of the path*
That he himself has made, O Sabhiya,
Is supremely serene
And beyond doubt.
He, who having given up
Both existence and non-existence,
Has lived the holy life
And is never again reborn —
He is the ***Bhikku.****"*

6. *"Always resigned,*
Indifferent to both
Pleasure and pain,
Mindful and never hurting anyone
In the entire world,
The monk,
Who has crossed the ocean,

Is untroubled
And not given to self-elevation —
He is ***humble.****"*

7. *"He whose sense faculties are developed*
Both inwardly and outwardly
In the whole world,
Who, having broken through
This world and the next,
Who being developed,
Awaits the time of death —
He is ***tamed.****"*

8. *"Having considered all ages,*
Having seen the cycle of Samsara —
The disappearance
And reappearance of life —
He is free from impurities,
Spotless and stainless.
He has attained
The destruction of becoming —
He is ***Enlightened.****"*

Then the wandering mendicant, who felt elated and overjoyed after hearing the Buddha's words, asked him another question:

9. *Sabhiya: "What should one accomplish to become a 'Brahmin'?*
When is one called a 'monk' (Samana)?
Why is one called 'washed-clean' (Nahataka)?
Why is one called 'faultless' (Naga)?
O Exalted One, explain this to me."

10. *The Buddha: "Having kept away from all evil,*
He is spotlessly clean,
Good, attentive and steadfast.
He is perfect
Since he has gone beyond Samsara —

Such an unattached person is termed
***A Brahmin.*"**

11. *"Quiet,*
Having transcended
Both good and evil,
Being free from corruption,
Having understood
This world and the next,
He has gone beyond birth and death —
Such a person is correctly called
***A monk.*"**

12. *"Purified of all evil*
Both inwardly and outwardly
In the whole world,
He does not get entangled
In the web
Of time-enslaved gods and men —
Such a person is termed
***Washed-clean.*"**

13. Then Sabhiya, who was feeling extremely happy, posed another question:

14. Sabhiya: "Whom do the Buddhas term 'winner of the field' (Khettajina)?
Why is one called 'virtuous' (Kusala)?
Why is one called 'wise' (Pandita)?
Why is one called 'sage' (Muni)?
O Exalted One, explain this to me."

15. *The Buddha: "Having examined all fields —*
The divine field,
The human field
And the Brahma field,
He is liberated
From the bond of all fields —

Such a person is called
Winner of the field."

16. *"Having examined all treasuries —*
The divine treasury,
The human treasury
And the Brahma treasury,
He is liberated
From the bond of all treasuries —
Such a person is called
Virtuous."

17. *"Having discerned*
The dual sense-fields,
The inner and the outer,
Having purity and intelligence,
He has transcended
Both good and evil —
Such a person is called
Wise."

18. *"Having understood*
The nature of the real
And the unreal,
Both within and without
In the entire world,
He is worthy of honour
By gods and men
For he has extricated himself
From the net of attachment —
Such a person is called
Sage."

Then the highly elated Sabhiya asked the following question:

19. Sabhiya: "When is a person called 'accomplished in knowledge' (Vedagu)?

When is a person called 'one who knows well' (Anuvidita)

and 'energetic' (Viriyava) ? Why is one named 'well-bred' (Ajaniya)?"

20. *The Buddha: "Having mastered all sensations,*
O Sabhiya,
That are known to ascetics
And Brahmins,
And being free
From human passion,
He is accomplished in knowledge."

21. *"Understanding well the delusion*
Of name and form
Both within and without,
Which is the root of all ills,
And being liberated
From the bond of all ills,
He is called
The one who knows well."

22. *"Keeping oneself*
From all evils in this world,
And passing beyond
The suffering of hell,
One becomes a house of energy.
Being full of energy and exertion,
Such a person is termed
Resolute."

23. *"He whose bonds are broken*
Both inside and outside,
And released
From the very root of all clinging,
Such a person is called
Well-bred."

Then the jubilant wanderer proceeded with another question.

24. Sabhiya: "When is a person called 'well versed in sacred learning' (Sottiya)?

    When is one called 'noble' (Ariya) and 'one of good conduct' (Caranavant)?

    Who is a 'wandering religious mendicant' (Paribbajako)? O Exalted One, explain this to me."

25. *The Buddha: "Having heard and understood*
    Every teaching in the world,
    Be it blameful or blameless.
    He is the victorious one
    Who is free from doubt,
    Entirely emancipated
    And free from suffering
    In every respect.
    Such a person is termed
    Well versed in sacred learning."

26. *"The wise person,*
    Having terminated
    His Asavas (biases)
    And attachments,
    Never again gets reborn in a womb.
    With the removal
    Of the threefold perceptions
    And the extrication of oneself
    From the mud of sensuality,
    He discovers the timeless.
    Such a person is termed
    Noble."

27. *"Whoever on earth*
    Has obtained the highest gain
    As regards good conduct
    Is always virtuous
    And understands the Dharma.

Being emancipated,
He is free from clinging
And free from aversions.
Such a person is termed
One of good conduct."

28. "*Shunning any action*
That results in pain,
Be it above, below, across or in between,
He has no deceit, conceit,
Greed and anger.
He has also put an end to
Name-and-form.
Such a person is termed
A wandering religious mendicant."

Thereupon Sabhiya, who was delighted and elated after hearing the Master's words, rose from his seat and reverentially saluted him with clasped hands.

29. Sabhiya: "You of great wisdom, who discarded the three and sixty sense-based heresies of ascetics, and went beyond the darkness of the flood!"

30. "You have gone to the end and you are beyond the reach of suffering. You are a worthy man, the fully Enlightened One.

    I regard you as one who has transcended his passions. Brilliant, wise and rich in intelligence, you have carried me across."

31. "After learning about my uncertainty, you have carried me across. Homage to you, O Sage who has obtained the highest. Kinsman of the Sun, you are gentle!"

32. "You have cleared my previous doubts, O Seer. Truly you are a Sage (*Muni*), perfectly Enlightened, who has overcome the obstacles."

33. "All your disturbances have come to an end. You are tranquil, tamed, courageous and truthful."

34. "You are the faultless among the faultless (*Naganagassa*) and the great hero. All the celestial beings, including Narada and Pabbata, rejoice when they hear you speaking."

35. "Praise be to you, O distinguished individual! Praise be to you, O greatest of men! In the world of gods and men you remain unrivalled."

36. "You are the Awakened One, You are the Teacher, the Sage who overcame Mara! Having removed the latent tendencies, you have gone beyond and taught others to do so."

37. "You have overcome the substratum of clinging (Upadhi). The cankers (Asavas) have all been destroyed. You are the unattached and fearless lion!"

38. "The white and lovely lotus flower remains undefiled in the water. Likewise, you do not cling either to good or evil. O hero, stretch out your feet for Sabhiya venerates them!"

The wandering ascetic fell at the Master's feet and took refuge in the Buddha, the Dharma and the Sangha. Sabhiya made a request for the robe and orders. The Buddha granted his request. Next, the new monk led not only a solitary life but also one that was strenuous and energetic. Before long, by his own understanding, Sabhiya became an Arhat.

8

Rare is the Sight of a Buddha

The Buddhist scriptures abound with references to ascetics, hermits and monks. At the outset of the **Selasutta,** which we shall presently consider, one comes across a *jatilo* (an ascetic with long matted hair).

Once the Buddha and a great many monks, numbering twelve hundred and fifty, were touring in the Anga country north of the famous Ganges River. He arrived in the market-town of Apana. When he was staying there a certain mat-haired ascetic, by the name of Keniya, was very pleased to learn of the Master's presence in their midst.

Among other favourable details, the ascetic heard that the fully Enlightened One, this teacher of gods and men, not only taught the noble and profound Dharma but also advocated the leading of a perfectly pure life. How good, he thought, is the sight of such saints!

Then Keniya went up to the Sage and they exchanged greetings. As a result of listening to a discourse of the Buddha, the ascetic was fired with enthusiasm. Thereupon Keniya extended to him an invitation.

Keniya: "May the good Gotama along with the monks accept from me a meal tomorrow?"

The Buddha: "Great indeed
Is the assembly of monks.
Besides, you are a follower
Of the Brahmins!"

For the second time Keniya extended his invitation but the Master replied as before and thereby indicated his refusal. But when the invitation was extended for the third time the Buddha agreed by remaining silent.

Often it was the case that the Buddha expressed his willingness to do something or allow something only after someone had submitted a proposal or made a request for the third time in succession. One can endlessly speculate about the reasons for his yielding to others' demands at the third attempt, after having turned down the two preceding ones. Those who dabble in the occult might believe that there is something sacrosanct about the odd number three. Be that as it may, for are our conditioned minds ever capable of successfully fathoming the mysterious depths of a liberated individual? However, there is a simple explanation. When devotees untiringly persist in inviting the Buddha, are not such deeds evidence of a certain seriousness and sincerity? Does not such eagerness also suggest the probable existence of an abiding interest in the Dharma? Moreover, when devotees have to reconcile themselves to the unpleasantness of these refusals, their *Saddha* (faith) is, as it were, put to the test. After trying again for the third time, they have, as it were, passed the test.

After returning to his hermitage, Keniya assembled together his servants, friends and relations. Next he informed them about the forthcoming meal. He sought their help and they readily agreed to render it. Soon they set about digging fire-pits, splitting firewood, washing pots and pans, providing jars of water and arranging seats. Keniya himself prepared a circular pavilion.

Keniya was an ardent follower of a very erudite Brahmin called Sela who was living in Apana. Such was the extent of Sela's learning that he had even mastered the three Vedas. Skilled in metre and grammar, and proficient in metaphysical theories, Sela was described as having "the signs of a great man". He taught hymns to a group of young men.

When in the course of their wanderings Sela and his three hundred young men visited the hermitage of Keniya, Sela noticed that the place was a hive of activity.

Sela: "Is the Venerable Keniya making preparations for the marriage of a son or daughter? Are you going to have a sacrifice, or has Bimbisara, the king of Magadha, along with his army been invited for tomorrow's meal?"

Keniya: "No, Sela, neither will there be a wedding feast nor a royal visitor, yet elaborate preparations are being made for a great sacrifice. The recluse Gotama has arrived at Apana. This Gotama is held in high repute. They say that he is Lord Buddha. I have invited him and his community of monks for tomorrow's meal."

Sela: "Did you say that he is a Buddha?"

Keniya: "Yes, I say that he is a Buddha."

Sela: "Did you say that he is a Buddha?"

Keniya: "Yes, I say that he is a Buddha."

Then the Brahmin Sela started thinking as follows: "Even the word 'Buddha' is hardly heard in the world. Our hymns have handed down the thirty-two characteristics of a great being. Only two courses are open to one with these signs. Should he lead the life of a householder, he will become the Emperor of the four quarters of the earth, a virtuous king who reigns righteously, a conqueror of the world, who secures stability in his land and possesses the seven gems. These are the wheel-gem, the elephant-gem, the horse-gem, the pearl-gem, the woman-gem, the householder-gem and the counsellor-gem. His sons are more than a thousand in number, who having great bodily strength and bravery, crush their enemies. Without violence he conquers the entire sea-surrounded earth and rules righteously, without resorting to the sword. But if he goes forth from home to homelessness, then he becomes an Arhat, an All-Enlightened One who removes the veil in the world."

Then Sela asked aloud: "Where is Gotama staying, this Arhat and All-Enlightened One?"

"Over there," replied Keniya, stretching out his right arm towards the blue forest line.

Sela, accompanied by these three hundred young men, proceeded to the Teacher. As they went Sela instructed them by saying, "Walk step by step without making any noise, for Buddhas, like solitary lions, are hard to approach. When I speak to him, do not interrupt me, but wait until the conversation is over."

Thereafter Sela approached the Teacher, greeted him and sat down at one side. While being seated Sela started looking for the thirty-two signs of a great being. He managed to see all the signs except two of them: namely, the male sexual organ being ensheathed and the very long tongue. Sela's doubtful mind was unclear about these matters. Then the Master manifested his psychic power. Consequently Sela saw that what was cloth-concealed was in fact sheath-enclosed. Furthermore, the Master put out his tongue and licked not only his ear-apertures but also his nostrils; next, with his tongue he covered his entire forehead.

Then the Brahmin Sela thought as follows: "The ascetic Gotama undoubtedly has all the thirty-two marks of greatness, not just some of them, yet I am not sure whether or not he is a

Buddha. But I have heard it said by aged Brahmins, teachers and the teachers of teachers that the Arhats, the fully Enlightened Ones, reveal themselves when they are praised. So I will praise Gotama." Then Sela, while facing the Buddha, uttered the following verses of eulogy:

1. "You are perfect in body, very pleasant, well-born and beautiful to behold. Gold-coloured with very white teeth, O Exalted One, you are full of vigour."
2. "Your body bears the marks of the highborn: the same signs as those of a great being."
3. "Bright-eyed, fair-faced, great, straight and majestic, in the midst of monks you shine like the sun."
4. "You are a gold-skinned and handsome monk. What is the use of being an ascetic when you have such beauty?"
5. "You deserve to be a wheel-turning king, a ruler of the four-cornered earth, a conqueror, the supreme lord of the Jambu (*Rose-apple*) Grove — India."
6. "Princes must be seen merely as your village-headmen, O Gotama, since you are the king of kings and ruler of mankind."
7. *The Buddha: "I am indeed a King, O Sela,*
The Supreme King
Of Dhammaraja (righteousness).
With the Dharma
I set the wheel turning,
Which none can roll back."
8. Sela: "You claim to be wholly awakened, a supreme king of righteousness. You say that with the Dharma you have set the wheel turning."
9. "Who is your general, the disciple, the devoted follower of the Teacher? Who after you will turn the wheel of Dharma that you have set turning?"

10. *The Buddha: "The incomparable wheel of Dharma*
That I have turned
Will be kept turning
By my faithful heir Sariputta."

11. *"What is to be known*
Has been known by me;
What is to be developed
Has been developed by me;
What has to be given up,
That I have done.
Therefore, O Brahmin,
I am a Buddha."

12. *"Discard your doubts about me*
And have faith, O Brahmin,
For rare is the sight
Of a Buddha."

13. *"Of those who are seldom seen*
In this world, O Brahmin,
I am one of them —
A fully awakened physician
Without an equal."

14. *"Having become a Brahmabhuta (divine being),*
The Incomparable Conqueror
Of Mara's armies,
Having defeated all foes
And being free from fear,
I rejoice."

15. Sela: "Listen to him, venerable sirs. As the one with supernatural insight says, he is the physician, the great hero, who like a lion roars in the forest."

16. "After seeing this divine being beyond compare, this conqueror of Mara's armies, who would not have faith in him, even if he were low-born?"

17. *"He who approves of me, let him follow me.*
 He who disapproves of me, let him depart.
 I go forth into homelessness under him of noble wisdom."

18. The Brahmin youths: "If the teaching of the fully Enlightened One pleases you, we shall also go forth into homelessness under him of noble wisdom."

19. Sela: "With outstretched hands these three hundred Brahmins beg of you, O Exalted One, to be allowed to lead the holy life under you."

20. *The Buddha: "That life,*
 So well preached,
 Is here and now,
 Yet it is timeless.
 The going forth
 Is not in vain
 For the vigilant."

Thereafter the Brahmin Sela and his followers received both the ordination and the higher ordination from the Buddha.

In the forenoon the Master robed himself and took his outer robe and begging-bowl. Accompanied by the monks, he went to Keniya's hermitage and sat in the seat prepared for him. With his own hands Keniya served his guests with a lot of hard and soft food until they refused to have any more. After the Master had finished his meal Keniya sat on one side. The Buddha expressed his thanks to his host with the following stanzas:

21. *The Buddha: "The foremost sacrifice*
 Is the fire-offering,
 The foremost of Vedic metres
 Is Savitri,
 The foremost of men

Is the king,
The foremost of rivers
Is the ocean."

22. *"The foremost of heavenly bodies*
Is the moon,
The foremost of burning bodies
Is the sun,
The foremost
Is the Order of Monks
For merit-orientated offerings."

After thanking Keniya, the Master rose from his seat and left.

Thereafter Sela and his followers led a life that was solitary, vigilant and ardent. Before long Sela attained the goal of the holy life and was numbered among the Arhats.

Sela went to visit the Buddha. With his palms outstretched towards the Exalted One in a gesture of adoration, Sela addressed him in the following stanzas:

23. *Sela and his followers: "We took refuge in you*
Eight days ago, O Seer,
And within a week
Your teaching has tamed us."

24. *"You are the Buddha,*
You are the Teacher,
Sage, Subduer of Mara,
Stream-crosser and helper."

25. *"Your defilements have dropped,*
Your taints have terminated.
Fearless, you are a lion
Without any attachments."

26. *"Three hundred monks stand here*
With outstretched palms.

Stretch out your feet
For the pure people
Wish to pay homage to them."

9

Why be Given to Grieving ?

The compassionate Buddha preached the **Salla Sutta** to console a devout patron. Such was the poor man's sorrow that he had starved himself for a week following the death of his son.

What is the special meaning of *Salla* (arrow) in Pali? This stinging arrow is craving or attachment. It pierces us all and is in need of removal.

1. *"The length of life*
   Of mortal man here on earth
   Is neither calculable nor known.
   His short life is difficult
   And entailed in suffering."

2. *'For there is no means by which*
   Anyone born
   Can avoid death.
   Old age is followed
   By death.
   Such is the nature
   Of living beings."

3. *"As with ripe fruits*
That are in danger of falling
In the morn,
So are mortals born
With the constant fear
Of death."

4. *"The potter's earthen vessels*
All end up
Being broken.
Likewise is the life of mortal man."

5. *"Both the young and the old,*
Both the foolish and the wise,
They are all completely
In death's power.
They will all end up
Dead."

6. *"Of those who,*
Having been surmounted by death,
Go across to the next world,
A father cannot rescue his son
Nor a relative his relations."

7. *"Mark my words,*
Even when the relations look on
And are in mourning,
Each and every mortal
Is like an ox
Taken for slaughter."

8. *"The world is troubled*
By decay and death.
Understanding
The nature of the world,
The wise
Are not given to grieving."

9. *"Not knowing the path*
From where they came
Or whereto they leave,
Not knowing either end,
You mourn
For no good reason or purpose."

10. *"If by grieving*
Any gain were possible,
The wise
Would have done likewise.
Only the foolish
Thus hurt themselves."

11. *"Not by weeping and sorrowing*
Does one find peace of mind,
But pains increase
And the body suffers."

12. *"Their self-inflicted pains*
Make mourners lean and pale,
And the dead get no protection.
Lamentations are of no avail."

13. *"Those who fail to drop grieving*
Suffer even more pain.
By wailing over the dead
They fall into grief's power."

14. *"Look at the rest*
Who also are going to leave,
The men who get their just deserts.
Fallen under death's sway,
The living are trembling with fear."

15. *"In whatever way man plans,*
It turns out differently.
It is very disappointing.

Such is the nature
Of this world!"

16. *"Even if a man were to live*
For a hundred years or even more,
He will still have to part company
From his relations
And cease living
In this world."

17. *"Therefore listen*
To the Arhat
And cease mourning.
On seeing a corpse,
One realises that
'Never again will I meet
That dead person'."

18. *"With water*
One puts out the fire
When a house is in flames.
Similarly, sorrow
Is cast off
By those who are wise,
Learned and skilful.
It drifts away
Like a tuft of cotton
In the wind."

19. *"The one who seeks happiness*
Should draw out his arrow
Of lamentation and sorrow
As well as greediness."

20. *"With the arrow drawn out,*
Being free from every attachment,
Finding calmness of mind,

And going beyond all sorrow,
One attains Nirvana."

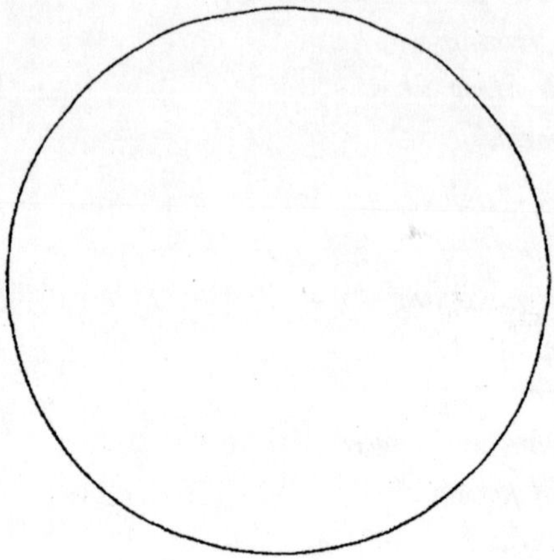

10

Brahmin by Birth or Brahmin by Deeds?

More than 2500 years ago the Buddha spoke against the birth-based caste system. The Brahmanical attitude of superiority towards other castes often met with resentment or resistance from the so-called low castes. The all-compassionate Buddha never disliked the Brahmins nor anyone for that matter, but the faith of the people in the time-honoured caste-system was seriously undermined by his new definition of "Brahmin". The theme of the **Vasetthasutta**, which we will deal with in due course, is that one becomes a Brahmin not by birth, but solely by one's deeds. This revolutionary approach to the caste system came as a shock to many, and it is reasonable to believe that this might well have been one of the principal reasons why the orthodox were so opposed to the Buddha and his teachings.

The hereditary four-fold caste system of ancient India might seem to be on the decline but it is, in truth, still part and parcel of modern Indian society. Although there is no longer a strict adherence to the rules of caste, it cannot be said that the socially divisive and disruptive caste system has altogether disappeared.

Caste consciousness frequently finds overt expression in the gross ill-treatment of the so-called inferiors by the so-called superiors. It is also often the case that caste-consciousness continues to be present covertly and subtly in many a psyche. But to be fair, the curse of caste is not confined to Hindu society. Is there any country in the world that is not plagued by caste? Called differently, the caste canker can be seen in operation in *every* society in disguise. Other societies categorically avoid using that loaded word "caste" when referring to their own various class-conscious groups — social classes based on beliefs, skin colour, education, wealth and so forth.

In essence, the caste mentality is there whenever a group of persons isolates itself by erecting social barriers, which means that so-called outsiders are debarred from joining that group. Whereas someone with a working-class background can someday belong to a higher social class by becoming very rich or by moving out of slummy surroundings into a wealthy neighbourhood, it is never possible to *change* the caste into which one is born. The element of social mobility that characterises the class system is deplorably lacking in the caste system. But in other respects, there is no fundamental difference between caste-consciousness and class-consciousness. Both these extremely self-centred forms of exclusivity can be found everywhere. This psychological malaise is an unfortunate feature of our world.

In the Indian social hierarchy, the Brahmins are right at the top. By tradition, Brahmins are usually pious persons of great erudition and their simple lifestyles underscore their otherworldliness. Often they go into teaching. Those Brahmins who become priests have a religious obligation to do their priestly duties. For these reasons the members of the other castes are expected to show the greatest respect for Brahmins.

Next in importance are the Kshatriyas who are involved in law making, law enforcing and military matters.

Despite the fact that he had been born into the governing high caste called Kshatriya, the Buddha did not identify himself with this caste nor with any other caste for that matter.

On the one hand the Buddha denounced the doctrines of the Brahmins, but on the other, he decided to call an Arhat a Brahmana. In the Buddhist scriptures the Buddha, the Paccekabuddhas and the Arhats are all termed Brahmanas. Those who are Brahmins by birth can be regarded as real Brahmins only if they become Brahmins by deeds. This means that even low caste persons and untouchables are entitled to that prestigious appellation "Brahmana", provided of course that they have attained Enlightenment.

Once when the Buddha was staying in the Icchanankala Forest, it so happened that many famous and wealthy Brahmins were also living in Icchanankala. While two young Brahmins, Vasettha and Bharadvaja, were walking up and down and exercising their limbs, they got into a casual conversation. Their topic of discussion was "how does one become a Brahmin?"

Bharadvaja: "When one is well-born on both the mother's side and that of the father, pure in descent for seven successive generations on both sides, and if the birth remains unchallenged and beyond reproach, then such a person is a Brahmin."

Vasettha: "A person is a Brahmin to the extent that he is virtuous and cares to observe the religious vows."

They examined this question together, but Bharadvaja failed to convince Vasettha nor Vasettha Bharadvaja. Then on the suggestion of Vasettha, Bharadvaja agreed to visit the recluse Gotama and ask him about this matter. Then the two young men met the Buddha, exchanged greetings and sat down apart.

1. Vasettha: "Others accept and acknowledge the fact that we are masters of the three Vedas. I am a young Brahmin student of Pokkharasati and this young Brahmin is a student of Tarukkha."

2. "We are experts in the three Vedas. Well versed in the texts, we are grammarians who can equal our teachers as regards recitation."
3. "Concerning the question of birth, we are in dispute, O Gotama. According to Bharadvaja one becomes a Brahmin by birth, but I say that it takes place by deeds. O Seer, know this to be so."
4. "As we are having this disagreement, we come here to ask you, for you are renowned as being fully Enlightened."
5. "As people with clasped hands raised high, adore the waxing moon, so the world pays homage to Gotama."
6. "We ask Gotama, the Eye of the World: Does one become a Brahmin by birth or by actions? Explain this to us so that we who are ignorant may discover a Brahmin."

7. *The Buddha: "O Vasettha,*
I will explain in the right order
The classification of species
Of living things.
Many are the species."

8. *"Observe the grass and the trees.*
They do not reason,
But their distinguishing feature
Arises from their species.
Many are their species."

9. *"Observe the worms, the moths*
And the different kinds of ants.
Their distinguishing feature
Arises from their species.
Many are their species."

8. *"Observe the four-footed animals,*
Both small and large.
Their distinguishing feature

Arises from their species.
Many are their species."

9. *"Observe the long-backed snakes*
That move on their bellies.
Their distinguishing feature
Arises from their species.
Many are their species."

10. *"Observe the fish*
That live in the water.
Their distinguishing feature
Arises from their species.
Many are their species."

11. *"Observe the winged birds*
That wander the skies.
Their distinguishing feature
Arises from their species.
Many are their species."

12. *"All these species*
Have many distinguishing features,
Separating each one from the others,
Whereas with man
His distinguishing marks
Are not many."

13. *"They differ not*
As regards their hair,
Head, ears, eyes, mouth, nose,
Lips nor eyebrows,

14. *"Nor as regards their neck,*
Shoulders, belly, back,
Chest and genitalia"

15. *"Nor as regards their hands,*
Feet, fingers, nails, carves, thighs,

Colour nor voice
Is there a distinguishing feature
As in other species."

16. *'No such bodily difference*
Can be found in any individual
Among men.
The difference among men
Is only in name."

17. *"The person who gains a livelihood*
By keeping cows
Is a farmer, not a Brahmin."

20. *"The person who gains a livelihood*
By practising a craft
Is an artisan, not a Brahmin."

21. *'The person who gains a livelihood*
By selling goods
Is a merchant, not a Brahmin."

22. *'The person who gains a livelihood*
By serving others
Is a servant, not a Brahmin."

23. *'The person who gains a livelihood*
By taking what has not been given to him
Is a thief, not a Brahmin."

24. *'The person who gains a livelihood*
By archery
Is a soldier, not a Brahmin."

25. *'The person who gains a livelihood*
By being a priest
Is a sacrificer, not a Brahmin."

26. *'The person who owns*
Villages and countries
Is a king, not a Brahmin."

27. *"Nor is a person a Brahmin*
By virtue of parentage.
He may be addressed as 'Sir'
As he is wealthy,
But the one who has nothing
And clings to nothing —
Him do I call a Brahmin."

28. *"The person, who*
Being free from all fetters,
Is fearless, desireless
And without ties —
Him do I call a Brahmin."

29. *"The Enlightened One*
Who has severed
The strap of anger,
The thong of desiring,
The cord of dogmatic views
And latent tendencies,
And has also cast aside
The crossbar of ignorance —
Him do I call a Brahmin."

30. *"The person who can patiently*
Endure reproach,
Torture and imprisonment,
And whose forbearance is strong,
Which is his army —
Him do I call a Brahmin."

31. *"Resentment-removed,*
Observant of religious duties,
Virtuous, free from pride
And restrained,
The person

Who bears his final body —
Him do I call a Brahmin."

32. *"Like water on a lotus leaf*
Or a mustard seed on the tip of a needle,
The person
Who does not hold onto
Sensual pleasures —
Him do I call a Brahmin."

33. *"The person*
Who understands
Here and now
The ending of suffering,
Who casts off his burden
And is hence liberated —
Him do I call a Brahmin."

34. *"The person*
Whose wisdom is profound,
Who is intelligent,
Who knows the right path
From the wrong,
And who has attained
The Highest —
Him do I call a Brahmin."

35. *"The person*
Who isolates himself
From both the home-dwellers
And the homeless,
Who is free from attachment
And frugal —
Him do I call a Brahmin."

36. *"The person*
Who lays aside
Cruelty towards creatures,

Those that tremble
And those that are strong,
Neither killing them
Nor causing them
To be killed —
Him do I call a Brahmin."

37. *"The person*
Who is not hostile
Amidst the hostile,
Serene amidst the violent
And free from attachments
Amidst those who have them —
Him do I call a Brahmin."

38. *"The person*
Whose greed, hate,
Conceit and hypocrisy
Have all fallen down,
Like a fallen mustard seed
From the point of a needle —
Him do I call a Brahmin."

39. *"The person*
Who gives expression
To truthful, gentle
And instructive words
That are not offensive to anyone —
Him do I call a Brahmin."

40. *"The person*
Who does not take for himself
That which was not given to him,
Whether it be long or short,
Small or large,
Good or bad —
Him do I call a Brahmin."

41. *"The person*
Who longs not for anything
Of this world
Nor the hereafter,
Who is desireless
And unfettered —
Him do I call a Brahmin."

42. *"The attachment-free person,*
Who by means of knowledge
Becomes doubt-free
And dives into the depths
Of ambrosial immortality —
Him do I call a Brahmin."

43. *"Having gone beyond*
Both good and bad,
Thus having escaped
From both bonds,
The person
Who is sorrowless,
Stainless and pure —
Him do I call a Brahmin."

44. *"The person*
Whose craving for rebirth
Has come to an end,
Is like a spotless moon:
Pure, clear
And undisturbed —
Him do I call a Brahmin."

45. *"He has crossed over the road*
That is beset with moral depravities,
Which is difficult to pass,
And gone to Yonder Shore.
Having transcended delusion,

He is meditative,
Desireless and doubt-free.
This person has attained
Craving-free calm —
Him do I call a Brahmin."

46. *'The person*
Who entirely gives up
The pursuit of sensual pleasures
In this world
And wanders about homelessly,
Devoid of the desire
For sensual pleasures
And bereft of becoming —
Him do I call a Brahmin."

47. *'The person*
Who entirely gives up
Craving
In this world
And wanders about homelessly,
Devoid of craving
And bereft of becoming —
Him do I call a Brahmin."

48. *'The person*
Who renounces
Human attachment,
Transcends divine attachment,
And finds release
From **all** *attachments —*
Him do I call a Brahmin."

49. *'The person*
Who has abandoned
Both attachment
And non-attachment,

Hence tranquil
And free from the elements
Of existence,
Is a hero who overcomes
The entire world —
Him do I call a Brahmin."

50. *"The person*
Who knows from beginning to end
The passing away of beings
And their rebirth,
The non-attached Well-Farer
Who is Enlightened —
Him do I call a Brahmin."

51. *"The person*
Whose journey
Remains unknown
To the deities,
The class of demigods
Called Gandhabbas
And humans,
The Arhat
Whose taints have terminated —
Him do I call a Brahmin."

52. *"The person*
For whom there is
Nothing whatsoever
In the past,
Nor the future,
Nor the period in-between,
Hence he is not given to grasping —
Him do I call a Brahmin."

53. *"This bull of a man,*
This noble hero,

This great saint,
This victorious one
Who is desireless, cleansed
And Enlightened —
Him do I call a Brahmin."

54. *"The person*
Who remembers his past lives,
Who sees both heaven and hell,
And who has reached the ending
Of existence
Via Arhatship —
Him do I call a Brahmin."

55. *"What the world has termed*
'Name' and 'family'
Is merely nominal.
What has been so designated
Here and there
Is the outcome
Of common consent."

56. *"For a long time*
A misconception
Had lain dormant
In the ignorant.
They say that it is
By birth
That one becomes a Brahmin."

57. *"Not by birth*
Does one become a Brahmin.
Not by birth
Does one become a non-Brahmin.
It is one's actions
That make one a Brahmin.
It is one's actions

That make one a non-Brahmin."

58. *"By deeds*
One becomes a farmer
And by deeds
An artisan, a merchant
Or a servant."

59. *"It is by deeds*
That one becomes a robber too,
By deeds
A soldier, a sacrificial priest
Or a king."

60. *"Thus the wise,*
Understanding
The chain of causation,
Well aware
Of the fruit of action (retribution),
Seeing what happened before
And what followed therefrom,
See action correctly."

61. *"It is by action*
That the world goes on,
It is by action
That living beings go on.
As a moving chariot wheel
Is bound by its linchpin,
So are beings
Bound by action
And kept shackled."

62. *"By means of austerity, chastity,*
Abstinence and tameness
One becomes a Brahmin.
This is the highest
State of Brahminhood."

63. *'The person*
With the threefold higher knowledge —
Anicca (Impermanence),
Dukkha (Suffering)
And Anatta (Egolessness) —
Is calm,
And his cycle of rebirths
Has ceased.
Know, O Vasettha,
That to those with understanding,
Such a person
Is Sakka and Brahma."

At the conclusion of this long discourse the two Brahmin youths Vasettha and Bharadvaja, who had been the listeners, declared: "It is excellent... we take refuge in Gotama, his Dharma and the order of monks. May you regard us as your lay disciples from now until the end of our days."

On a later occasion the Buddha preached to Vasettha the *Tevijja Sutta*. Before long he became a monk. After his listening to the *Agganna Sutta* Vasettha was given the higher ordination. Thereafter he became an Arhat. This detail is all the more interesting because in the *Vasettha Sutta* the Master had made it abundantly clear that only Arhats are genuine Brahmins.

In this remarkable story someone who was a Brahmin by name only suddenly blossoms into an Arhat or an authentic Brahmin.

11

The Hidden Danger in Slander

The improper conduct of the monk Kokaliya was the occasion for the preaching of the **Kokaliyasutta,** which we shall be considering in due course.

It is not only eminently worthwhile but also very interesting to have a good idea of the particular circumstances surrounding the delivery of this discourse or indeed any discourse for that matter. Therefore, at the beginning of this investigation, it will be helpful to take into account the following facts that provide some insight into Kokaliya's character.

Kokaliya used to live in the monastery constructed by his father in Kokali. On one occasion the two foremost disciples of the Buddha, namely Sariputta and Moggallana, spent the rainy season with Kokaliya as they were keen on staying in quiet surroundings. They did so because Kokaliya had promised them not to divulge their whereabouts. However, at the end of the rainy period, when the two disciples were about to leave, Kokaliya committed the faux pas of telling the townsfolk of their stay, and he then proceeded to scold the people. He made the accusation that they had not been hospitable to the two distinguished disciples Sariputta and Moggallana. The people reacted by rushing to these two disciples and presenting them with gifts, which they turned down. The monk Kokaliya was upset that the people failed to present him with gifts for that had been his expectation.

The two disciples undertook to return to these eager people sometime in the future. They kept to their word. When the disciples and a large number of monks returned to the town they were received as honoured guests. This time the gifts that were offered them were divided among the monks but poor monk Kokaliya received nothing. Kokaliya started using abusive language. The disciples went away. The situation provoked an angry response from the laity, who stated that Kokaliya must either fetch Sariputta and Moggallana or leave the place himself! But the two disciples were not at all interested in returning. Thereupon Kokaliya gave vent to his anger by going to the Buddha and speaking ill of Sariputta and Moggallana.

In the light of the foregoing information, we can now consider this sutta.

Once when the Lord was in residence in Jeta's Grove in Anathapindika's monastery at Savatthi, Kokaliya visited him as already explained. The visitor saluted him, sat down on one side, and made slanderous remarks.

Kokaliya: "Sariputta and Moggallana, Sir, are full of evil desires. It is evil that drives them on."

The Buddha: "Do not say so, Kokaliya.
Do not say so, Kokaliya.
Do not harbour such feelings
Against Sariputta and Moggallana
For they have a friendly nature."

Thrice did Kokaliya make these accusations and thrice did the Buddha give the same answer.

Then the monk Kokaliya, after rising from his seat, saluted the Lord, walked round him in a clockwise direction as a mark of respect, and then left the place.

Soon afterwards all over the body of Kokaliya blister-like swellings arose. At first these swellings were of the size of mustard seeds; they grew and enlarged to the size of lentils; then to the size of chick-peas; then to that of jujube's kernels, and later to that of jujubes. The growing continued to the size of myrobalans, then to the size of vilva fruits, and finally to the size of quinces. At that stage there was a discharge of pus and blood. Eventually, the monk passed away. Kokaliya, who had harboured hostility towards Sariputta and Moggallana, was reborn in the Paduma hell.

Illuminating the entire Jeta's Grove with the sheer effulgence of his body late in the night, Brahma Sahampati visited the Master and made a statement.

Brahma Sahampati: "The monk Kokaliya has been reborn in the Paduma hell on account of his hostile thoughts."

Then at the end of the night the Buddha addressed the monks and conveyed to them the message from Brahma Sahampati relating to Kokaliya's rebirth.

A monk: "What will be the length of time that he will have to stay in the Paduma Purgatory?"

The Buddha: "Long, O monk,
Will be the duration
Of his stay.
It is difficult to calculate it
As being so many years,
Hundreds of years,
Thousands of years
Or hundreds of thousands of years."

A monk: "But is it possible to make a comparison?"

The Buddha: "Yes, it is possible.
Suppose there were a cartload
Of twenty Kosalan measures
Of sesame seeds

From which a man removes
Just one seed
At the end of every century;
Consequently the stock of seeds
Continues to lessen
And eventually
Not a single seed is left.
Well, more quickly
Would that stock come to an end
Than the duration
Of only one term in Abbuda hell!
O monk,
Just as twenty terms in Abbuda hell
Are equivalent to
One term in Nirabbuda hell;
Just as twenty terms in Nirabbuda hell
Are equivalent to
One term in Ababa hell;
Just as twenty terms in Ababa hell
Are equivalent to
One term in Ahaha hell;
Just as twenty terms in Ahaha hell
Are equivalent to
One term in Atata hell;
Just as twenty terms in Atata hell
Are equivalent to
One term in Kamuda hell;
Just as twenty terms in Kamuda hell
Are equivalent to
One term in Sogandhika hell;
Just as twenty terms in Sogandhika hell
Are equivalent to
One term in Uppalaka hell;
Just as twenty terms in Uppalaka hell
Are equivalent to

One term in Pundarika hell;
Just as twenty terms in Pundarika hell
Are equivalent to
One term in Paduma hell,
So is the very long duration
In Paduma hell.
This is where Kokaliya
Has been reborn
For having hardened his heart
Against Sariputta and Moggallana."

In this way did the Exalted One speak. Thereafter the One Who Walks Well (*Sugato*) spoke again.

1. *The Buddha: "Within the mouth of man*
Is born an axe at birth
With which the fool
Destroys himself
By giving expression
To ill-spoken words."

2. *"When one praises*
The blameworthy,
Or blames
The praiseworthy,
Evil collects in the mouth,
And there is no happiness."

3. *"Of such small value*
Is the loss of riches at dice,
Even losing all the possessions
And losing one's own self!
Because a far greater loss
Is bearing ill-will toward those
Who have gone to goodness."

4. *"The one who maligns*
The noble ones,

By directing his evil mind
And evil speech
Against them,
Finds himself in hell
For one hundred thousand and thirty-six terms
In Nirabbuda hell
And five terms in Abbuda hell."

5. *"The liar goes to hell,*
And so does the doer of a deed
Who later says 'I did not do it'.
Their fate will be alike
In the hereafter."

6. *"When a fool wrongs*
An innocent and pure person,
His evil deed
Rebounds on him,
Like the fine dust
Flung against the wind."

7. *"Whoever is enslaved by greed,*
Such a person
Uses abusive language
And condemns others,
He is without faith,
Stingy, unfriendly, selfish
And prone to backbiting."

8. *"O foul-mouthed, false*
And ignoble man,
Destroyer of beings,
Evil-doer, sinner,
You wicked and base-born man,
Do not be talkative here
For you will suffer in hell!"

9. *"You scatter dirt*
Over yourself,
For you scold the virtuous
While being a wrong-doer.
As you are guilty of misconduct,
You will fall
Into the pit of hell
And remain there
For a long time."

10. *"Nobody's action disappears;*
It surely comes back.
Only its doer receives it.
The wrong-doer, being stupid,
Experiences the pain himself
In the next life."

11. *"He arrives at the iron stake*
Where iron rods strike him.
The food eaten there is like
Red hot balls of iron."

12. *"Unpleasant is the speech*
Of the hell-keepers
Who talk to him.
The hell-dwellers
Do not approach him.
It is not a place of refuge.
They lie on embers and enter
A pyre in flames."

13. *"The wardens of hell*
Cover them with a net
And thrash them
With iron hammers.
The hell-dwellers then pass into
A dense dark fog that is
Endlessly vast."

14. *"Next they enter*
A blazing metal cauldron
Which is at boiling point
For a long time
As they bob up and down."

15. *"The evil doer simmers*
In a mixture of blood and pus.
He turns here and there.
Whatever he comes into contact with,
There he festers."

16. *"In worm-contaminated water*
The evil-doer stews.
It is not possible to flee from there
For all the surrounding cauldrons
Are the same."

17. *"When the hell-dwellers enter*
The Asipatta Forest
With its sharp sword-leaves,
Their limbs are cut into pieces.
Then the hell-keepers with hooks
Pull the tongues of wrong-doers
Forwards and backwards."

18. *"Next they arrive at Vetarani*
With its razor-sharp streams,
Hence difficult to cross.
The foolish wrong-doers
Fall into it."

19. *"While they are weeping there,*
They become the food
Of flocks of ravens, dogs,
Jackals and vultures.
Hawks and crows tear them apart."

20. *"Painful indeed is life in hell*
For wrong-doers.
So let a person
For the rest of his life
In this world do his duties
And not be intoxicated."

21. *"By means of those sesame seeds,*
The wise have counted the term
Of those in Paduma hell,
Which comes to five crores,
And twelve hundred crores in addition."

22. *"Such are the sufferings in hells!*
Such are the terms to be spent!
Therefore when in the midst of the pure,
The amiable and the good,
Constantly watch
Both your speech and your mind."

12

Leading the Life of a Recluse

What are the distinguishing or identifying features of a supreme sage? By carefully reading the **Nalakasutta,** which is a discourse on the exalted state of a sage, we can have some knowledge of this important question. One realises, of course, that merely knowing the contents of a sutta is not the same as understanding it profoundly, let alone actually living the Dharma in our daily lives in the light of that understanding.

Only a week following his famous first sermon to the first five disciples at Sarnath, the Buddha preached to Nalaka, the nephew of Asita.

The aged sage Asita was the teacher of King Suddhodana, the father of the Buddha-to-be. In accordance with ancient Sakyan custom, the king was given to treating his guru Asita with great respect. Asita renounced the world and started practising austerities. Asita developed supernatural powers (*Iddhi*) with the result that he was capable of spending the day in celestial worlds. Once when he was in the Tavatimsa celestial world, he noticed its festive atmosphere. Tavatimsa was decorated, and for the celestial beings it was a time of great rejoicing. Thereupon Asita inquired into the matter. He was extremely happy to know that the celestial beings were celebrating the birth of no other than that of Siddhartha Gautama in planet Earth.

Asita rushed to the palace and asked to see the newborn baby. When the king lifted the baby towards Asita for the infant to pay his respects to the visiting ascetic, something happened and everyone present was taken by surprise. For the tiny infant's legs suddenly turned and proceeded to rest on the matted hair of Asita! This action on the baby's part is traditionally interpreted as follows: there is none who is worthy of a Bodhisattva's reverence. On account of the Bodhisattva's obvious superiority over all other beings in the Samsaric process, as well as his exalted status, everyone is expected to pay his respects to him, whereas the Bodhisattva on his part is not required to pay obeisance to anyone.

Having noticed the auspicious signs on the baby's body, Asita realised that the prince was destined to attain Enlightenment. Although Asita was very pleased, he was also very sad. Asita wept because he knew that he would not live long enough to hear with his own ears the words of the Buddha when the latter would be preaching. Asita's premonition was that he would never hear the Master discoursing, for the reason that before long he was going to die and be reborn as a formless being in an *Arupa* (formless) world. Therefore Asita ordained his nephew Nalaka, hoping that Nalaka in the fullness of time might take advantage of the Buddha's teachings.

1. At noontide the holy sage Asita saw the cheerful group of thirty Tavatimsa gods who were intensely joyful. After praising Indra, these immaculately clad gods were singing and merrily waving their garments.
2. Noticing the high-spirited behaviour of the gods, Asita paid his respects to them.

   Asita: "Why are you so happy? Why are you twirling your clothes in festive mood?"

3. "Even when the gods emerged triumphant in their battle with the Asuras, even following the defeat of the Asuras, such excitement has not been seen. What extraordinary discovery makes the devas delighted?"

4. "They shout, sing and play musical instruments; they clap and dance! O residents of Mount Meru, I ask you to dispel my doubts quickly, O venerable ones!"

5. The Devas: "The Buddha-to-be, the incomparable gem, has been born in the world of men, for their happiness and welfare, in the village of Lumbini in the Sakyan country. So we are very happy and excessively pleased."

6. "He is the noblest person, the best of beings, the lord of men and the greatest of creatures. With a lionlike roar he will start turning the Wheel in the Rishi Forest."

7. Having heard this, Asita descended from Tusita, and rushed to Suddhodana's palace. He seated himself and asked the Sakyans a question.

   Asita: "Where is the young prince whom I am eager to see?"

8. The Sakyans showed their newborn son to the Sage Asita. The son was glistening with a golden sheen. It was like the golden creation of a craftsman from a fiery furnace, glorious and beautiful to behold.

9. Looking at the prince, bright like a flame, pure as the moon and stars in the skies, shining like the autumnal sun in the cloudless heavens, Asita went into raptures.

10. Although the gods were holding high up in the air a parasol with many ribs and circles, and yak-tail fans with golden handles were waving up and down, yet none could be seen doing the holding or waving!

11. On seeing the white parasol held high above the infant, who seemed like a golden ornament upon a blanket, the

ascetic with matted hair — the sage Kanhasiri (also known as Asita) received him with great delight.

12. Asita who had mastered the knowledge of marks and signs, and knew Vedic mantras in addition, held in his arms the bull among the Sakyans, and then in a loud voice gave an exclamation of great gladness.

    Asita: "None can equal him! He is supreme among men!"

13. Then remembering the imminence of his own death, Asita was so unhappy that he started shedding tears. The Sakyans saw the seer weeping.

    The Sakyans: "Why, will problems beset the prince?"

14. Asita noticed that the Sakyans were crestfallen.

    Asita: "No harm will befall the prince. I see no danger. Be glad that he is no ordinary being. Listen carefully to what I say!"

15. "The summit of Enlightenment this prince will attain. Having perceived the pinnacle of purity, out of compassionate concern for the welfare of the many, he will set in motion the wheel of the Dharma. The life of celibacy taught by him will spread far and wide."

16. "My lifespan is fast approaching its end. My death will take place and I shall not live to hear the Dharma of the one with a unique task. Therefore I am distressed, ruined and in pain."

17. To the great delight of the Sakyans, the holy Asita left the royal precincts to lead the religious life. Out of compassion for his own nephew, Asita was instrumental in introducing him to the Dharma of the one with a unique task.

18. Asita: "When you hear others use the word 'Buddha', who attained Enlightenment and trod the path of the Dharma, then go there, ask him about the teachings and lead the life of celibacy under the Exalted One."

19. Thus advised by the well-disposed thoughts of this pure seer-to-be, Ṅalaka awaited the Conqueror with a mass of merit and watchful sense-faculties.

20. Having heard that the Conqueror had set in motion the wheel of the Dharma, he went to see the Seer of seers. As the prophecy of Asita had come to pass, he asked:

    "What are the makings of a Sage?"

21. Nalaka: "Asita's forecast has proved to be correct. Therefore we ask you this, O Gotama, you who have gone to that yonder shore."

22. "O Great Sage (*Muni*), as I am homeless and wish to lead the life of a monk, explain to me the highest wisdom."

23. *The Buddha: "I will tell you of*
    The highest wisdom
    That is hard to find
    And difficult to follow.
    Yet I will explain it to you.
    Stiffen yourself, be strong!"

24. *"Let there be*
    Evenness of mind
    In the face of both
    Praise and blame.
    By being watchful of both
    Pride and hate
    One comes by calmness."

25. *"High thoughts and low thoughts*
    Flicker like flames in a forest.
    Women seduce the sage.
    Let them not tempt you!"

26. *"Let one avoid*
    Sexual intercourse,
    Leave behind

Sensual pleasures of all kinds,
And be neither hostile
Nor attached
To living creatures
Both weak and strong."

27. "*'I am like them: they are like me'—*
Viewing it in this way,
Doing as one would be done by,
Let a person
Neither kill
Nor cause others to do the killing."

28. "*By dropping the desires and greed*
Of ordinary men,
The one with insight
Manages to cross over this hell."

29. "*With food taken in moderation,*
Having few needs,
Devoid of covetousness,
Desireless and being free from craving,
He is happy and serene."

30. "*Having gone about in search of alms,*
The sage goes to a forest
And sits at the root of a tree."

31. "*Being keen on meditation,*
The sage in his wisdom
Takes delight in the depths of a forest
Where he meditates by the base of a tree."

32. "*When the night is no more, at dawn*
He goes to the outskirts of a village.
There he does not rejoice in receiving
The offerings to him."

33. "*After going to a village*
The sage does not rush

From house to house.
Avoiding all talk relating to food,
He does not say anything
That is self-seeking."

34. "*With evenness of mind,*
Neither does he think
'What I have received is good!' nor
'How good that I did not receive it!'
With such equanimity
The sage returns to his tree."

35. "*Moving about from place to place*
With his alms-bowl in hand,
Seeming dumb
But not at all dumb,
The sage neither feels contempt
When a trifling gift is given him
Nor does he dislike its giver."

36. "*The Recluse has shown*
Several paths.
They do not go twice
To yonder shore.
Not even once
Can it be reached
By thought."

37. "*In the monk who is free*
From craving,
Who is cut off
From the stream,
Who is beyond
Both good and bad,
No fever can be found."

38. "*I will show you the path of the sage.*
Be like a razor's edge!

Press the tongue against the palate
And restrain the stomach!"

39. *"Let the mind be attachment-free.*
Let the recluse not think too much.
Free from the carrion stench
Of defilements,
Remaining unattached,
It is his aim to lead
A celibate life."

40. *"He must train himself to live alone.*
Solitude is synonymous with wisdom.
It is in solitude
That the sage finds delight."

41. *"You are going to shine forth*
In the ten directions.
After hearing the voices of approval
From the wise, from the meditators
And those who forewent their sensuality,
Let my disciple devote himself even more
To modesty."

42. *"Understand this!*
The waters from rivers, chasms and cracks
Gush forth noisily,
Whereas the waters of the mighty ocean
Move in silence."

43. *"What is empty makes a noise;*
Only what is full knows silence.
A half-filled pot, such is a fool:
A sage is akin to a complete pool."

44. *"When a recluse talks a lot*
That is possessed of good understanding,
He would be teaching the Dharma that he knows,

While being well aware
That he is talking a lot."

45. *"But he who,*
While knowing the Dharma,
Self-restrainedly does not speak much,
Such a Muni (Sage)
Is deserving of Sagehood.
He has in fact attained
Sagehood."

13

Dropping Our Defilements

Once the Lord was staying in the storeyed house of Migara's mother in Savatthi. On a full moon night he was seated in the open air. On that silent night the Master was surrounded by monks. When the Buddha looked around he noticed that all the monks were observing perfect silence.

In the mind's eye one can picture the idyllic calm that probably pervaded that place, where the Buddha preached the **Dvayatanupassanasutta**, or the discourse on the manner of viewing the *dyads* (groups of two).

The Buddha: "Monks, should anyone ask you:
'What is the use of listening
To these good, noble
And liberating teachings?'
You should answer:
'It is to understand
The dual teachings':

1. *'This is pain,*
   This is the origin of pain'.

2. *'This is the ending of pain,*
   This is the way leading to the ending of pain.'

When a monk in this manner
Fully understands the dyad,
He being vigilant, earnest and steadfast,
Reaps one of these two fruits —
Illumination immediately, or
The state of an Anagamin (Non-Returner),
If attachments still remain."

1. "*Those who do not understand suffering*
And its origin,
And the state wherein
Suffering has completely ceased
As well as the way
Leading to that cessation,"

2. "*they, failing to find*
The release of mind,
The release by means of wisdom,
Cannot make the ending.
They experience birth, old age,
Decay and death."

3. "*But those who understand suffering*
And its origin,
And the state wherein
Suffering has completely ceased
As well as the way
Leading to that cessation,"

4. "*they, finding the release of mind,*
The release by means of wisdom,
Succeed in making the ending.
They will not experience birth, old age,
Decay nor death."

"*Monks, if people were to ask:*
'Would it be right to look at the Dyad

In another manner?'
You should answer thus:"

"Whatever suffering arises,
It is all the consequence of
The Upadhis (elements of existence or
Substrata of rebirth)."

"With the total disappearance of
The elements of existence,
The arising of suffering
Comes to an end."

5. *"Whatever sufferings*
There are in this world,
Which are of many kinds,
They all originated in
The elements of existence.
The one who is ignorant of this fact
Creates the elements of existence,
And that fool suffers
Again and again.
Therefore the wise
Do not create
The elements of existence,
Having understood both
Birth and the origin of suffering."

"Whatever suffering arises,
It is all born of Avijja (ignorance).
With the total disappearance
Of ignorance,
The arising of suffering
Comes to an end."

6. *"Those who are trapped in Samsara*
(This cycle of continued existence)
With its succession of
Countless births and deaths —
This situation is caused
By ignorance."

7. *"For this ignorance*
Is the great foolishness,
Because of which
Beings have long been journeying
From birth to death
Again and again.
But those who come by knowledge
Are never reborn."

8. *"Whatever suffering arises,*
It is all born of Sankharas (karma-formations).
With the total disappearance
Of the karma-formations,
The arising of suffering
Comes to an end."

9. *"Seeing that this suffering*
Originates in karma-formations,
That the ending of karma-formations
And the stopping of perception
Will result in
The cessation of suffering,
Having understood this as it really is,"

10. *"The wise, with right vision,*
Having understood fully,
And having found release
From Mara's bonds,
Are no longer reborn."

11. *"Whatever suffering arises,*
It is all born of Vinnana (consciousness).
With the total disappearance
Of consciousness,
The arising of suffering
Comes to an end."

12. *"Seeing that this suffering*
Originates in consciousness,
With the cessation
Of consciousness
A monk, being desireless,
Is Parinibbuta (completely calmed)."

'Whatever suffering arises,
It is all born of Phassa (contact).
With the total disappearance
Of contact,
The arising of suffering
Comes to an end."

13. *"For those who are overpowered*
By contact
And caught in the stream
Of existence,
And who in addition follow
The wrong path,
The freedom from fetters will be
In the remote future."

14. *"But those who*
Comprehend contact,
Who know it well,
Who delight in
The cessation of contact,
They, being desireless,
Are completely calmed."

"Whatever suffering arises,
It is all born of Vedanas (sensations).
But with the total disappearance
Of sensations,
The arising of suffering
Comes to an end."

15. *"Everything that is sensed,*
Regardless of whether it is
Pleasant or unpleasant,
Neither pleasant nor unpleasant,
Experienced internally or externally,"

16. *"Seeing this to be suffering,*
Something delusory
And subject to decay,
And by repeatedly understanding
Its transitoriness,
One has detachment.
With the demise
Of sensations,
The desireless monk
Comes by complete calm."

"Whatever suffering arises,
It is all born of Tanha (craving).
But with the total disappearance
Of craving,
The arising of suffering
Comes to an end."

17. *"With the fever of craving*
As his companion,
He travels incessantly
From one form of existence
To another,

Never managing to go
Beyond Samsara (the round of rebirths)."

18. *"Out of the awareness*
That craving is the cause
Of suffering,
Being free from craving,
Without clinging,
The mindful monk
Walks around homelessly."

"Whatever suffering arises,
It is all born of Upadanas (clinging).
But with the total disappearance
Of clinging,
The arising of suffering
Comes to an end."

19. *"Clinging is the cause*
Of existence.
Anyone who comes into existence
Is subject to suffering.
Every birth is doomed
To end in death.
This is the origin of suffering."

20. *"Therefore, the wise*
Who end clinging,
Having perfectly understood
The ending of birth,
Never get reborn."

21. *"Whatever suffering arises,*
It is all born of Arambhas (exertions).
But with the total disappearance
Of exertions,
The arising of suffering
Comes to an end."

22. "*Seeing that suffering is caused*
By exertions,
Having given up exertions,
The monk who has found freedom
In non-exertion,"

23. "*Whose craving for existence ceased,*
Whose mind is calm,
Never again gets reborn."

24. "*Whatever suffering arises,*
It is all born of Ahara (sustenance).
But with the total disappearance
Of sustenance,
The arising of suffering
Comes to an end."

25. "*Seeing that suffering is caused*
By sustenance,
Realising the consequences
Of all forms of sustenance
And by not relying on any of them,"

26. "*Correctly perceiving*
That inward health is the outcome
Of casting aside the Asavas (cankers),
The reflective monk,
Being based in the Dharma,
Can no longer be regarded
As existing."

27. "*Whatever suffering arises,*
It is all born of Injita (movement).
But with the total disappearance
Of movement,
The arising of suffering
Comes to an end."

28. *"Seeing that suffering is caused*
By movement,
Therefore having given up movement,
Karma-formations having ended,
Being desireless,
Without clinging,
The mindful monk
Walks around homelessly."

29. *"Those who never depend,*
They never waver either.
But the ones who depend
Have to travel endlessly
From one form of existence
To another,
Never succeeding in transcending
Samsara (the round of rebirths)."

30. *"Seeing that suffering is caused*
By depending,
After giving up both
Depending and grasping,
The mindful monk
Walks around homelessly."

"Aruppa (the formless)
Is a calmer state
Than that with Rupa (form).
But calmer than the formless
Is cessation."

31. *"Beings with form*
And beings without form,
Unless they have understood
Cessation,
Will be liable to rebirth."

32. *"But those who have fully understood*
Both form and formlessness,
And are liberated in cessation,
They succeed in leaving death behind."

'Monks, what has been considered as
'This is true' by the world,
Including the devas, Mara, beings,
Ascetics, Brahmins and men,
That has been well seen as
'This is false' by the worthy ones
By means of their wisdom."

'Monks, what has been considered as
'This is false' by the world,
Including the devas, Mara, beings,
Ascetics, Brahmins and men,
That has been well seen as
'This is true' by the worthy ones
By means of their wisdom."

33. *"Seeing a 'self'*
When there is none
In respect of name-and-form,
The world of gods and men
See as real
What is unreal!
They think it is true!"

34. *"In whatever manner*
They consider the matter,
It turns out otherwise.
For it is inherently false.
Whatever is fleeting
Is inherently false."

35. *"Nirvana is devoid*
Of any deceitful nature
And the worthy ones
Have discovered that to be true.
On account of their complete
Comprehension of the truth,
They are hankering-free
And serene."

"Monks, what has been considered
As 'happiness' by the world,
Including the devas, Mara, Brahman,
Brahmins and men,
That has been well seen
As 'suffering' by the worthy ones
By means of their wisdom."

"Monks, what has been considered
As 'suffering' by the world,
Including the devas, Mara, Brahman,
Brahmins and men,
That has been well seen
As 'happiness' by the worthy ones
By means of their wisdom."

36. *"Forms, sounds, tastes, smells,*
Tangible things and mental phenomena:
All these are pleasant only
When regarded as real and existing."

37. *"'These when present lead to happiness:*
When absent to unhappiness.'
Such is how gods and men do think!"

38. *"For the noble ones*
The breaking up of personality
Is happiness.

This view of those with right vision
Is diametrically opposed to
The whole world's view."

39. "*What others regard as happiness,*
The noble ones call it suffering.
What others regard as suffering,
The noble ones call it happiness.
This is difficult to understand!
The ignorant are confused!"

40. "*There is gloom for the shrouded*
And total darkness for the unseeing.
But for the virtuous
The light is unveiled.
Although it is near at hand,
Those who are ignorant
Of the Dharma
Fail to see it."

41. "*The Dharma eludes those*
Who hanker after existence,
Just floating along
With the stream of existence
And under the rule of Mara."

42. "*Who except the worthy ones*
Deserve the state
Of utter understanding
That is Nirvana?
Realising well this state
That is free of Asavas (taints),
They succeed
In attaining Liberation."

Thus spoke the Buddha. The monks heard his words with great rejoicing. While the Master was delivering his discourse sixty monks ceased clinging once and for all.

14

Saving Oneself from Drowning in Sensuality

The **Kamasutta** is very short in length but its message is of inestimable value. The *Kamasutta*, which strongly supports the avoidance of sensual pleasures, is very different from a much later work of about the third century AD entitled *The Kama Sutra* of Vatsyayana, which is a Sanskrit treatise on love-making. All forms of sense-based happiness, including sexual pleasures, are necessarily short-lived. These transitory delights are all a far cry from the transcendental calm that is the inevitable outcome of the demise of sorrow-laden sensuality.

1. "*When the sensual pleasure-loving person*
   Succeeds in gratifying his longings,
   He certainly becomes glad."

2. "*If those sensual pleasures*
   Were to decrease,
   That pleasure-desirer woula suffer
   As though pierced by a dart."

3. "*Whoever shuns sensual pleasures*
   As though he avoids trampling
   On a snake's head,

Such a person,
Being mindful,
No longer clings to earthly things."

4. *"Whoever is eagerly desirous of fields,*
Goods, gold, cows and horses,
Servants, women, relations
Or numerous sensual pleasures,"

5. *"Being overpowered by his weaknesses*
And destroyed by dangers,
Suffering enters into him,
In the same manner that waters
Enter into a broken ship."

6. *"Therefore a watchful person*
Must eschew sensual pleasures.
Casting them aside,
He crosses the stream,
In the same way as
One bales out one's boat
And reaches yonder shore."

15

Our Body is a Cave

In the **Guhatthakasutta** one can regard the body as a cave or den, for "Guha" means "cave" or "heart". Within this cave of a body we, alas, have permitted wild animals such as lust to live!

1. "*The man who clings*
   To the cave of his body
   With its many hidden defilements
   Is muddle-headed.
   Since sensual pleasures
   Are not easy to shed,
   He knows not
   The state of detachment."

2. "*Enslaved and driven*
   By desire,
   People pursue
   The pleasures of the world,
   Eager for future, past
   And current pleasures.
   From these
   They find it difficult
   To extricate themselves.

Their pleasures
Cannot be extricated
By others."

3. *"Eagerly desirous*
Of sensual pleasures,
Being addicted to them,
Being blindly in love with them,
Those mean men follow
The wrong path.
When brought face to face
With suffering,
They sadly say,
'What will become of us
In the afterlife?'"

4. *"So before it is too late*
Let a man train himself
Here and now:
'Knowing what is wrong
In the world,
I will avoid doing wrong.'
The wise say that
This life is short."

5. *"I observe in the world*
Trembling humans
Who crave for
Different forms of existence.
These poor people,
Who are keen on having
Repeated existences,
Lament when they are faced
With death."

6. *"See how they tremble*
In their self-consciousness,

In the manner of floundering fish
In a stream with a dearth of water!
Seeing this,
Let them live
Without self-centredness
And also without clinging
To forms of becoming
Or existences."

7. *"Having gone beyond the attachment*
For both extremes,
Having comprehended
Sensory contact
And dropped it,
Not being greedy,
Doing nothing
That would make him
Feel blameworthy,
The wise one clings neither
To what is seen nor heard."

8. *"Having understood*
Sensory perception
And dropped it,
The Muni (Sage)
Manages to cross over
The stream.
He is undefiled by grasping.
With the arrow taken out,
Being vigilant,
He has no craving
For this world
Or the hereafter."

16

Dropping All Philosophical Views

The message of the **Dutthatthakasutta** is that the Sage is truly free because, so to speak, he has said "goodbye and good riddance" to all philosophical systems.

1. *"Truly, some ill-wishers*
   Strongly disapprove of others
   Out of malice,
   And truthful persons
   Also censure others
   But only out of goodwill.
   But the Sage
   Keeps himself aloof
   From disputes,
   Hence he has
   No mental obstruction whatsoever."

2. *"How can a desire-driven*
   And inclinations-enslaved man
   Ever go beyond
   His wrong views?
   For he would speak only
   According to the limits
   Of his knowledge."

3. "*When a man,*
Even unasked,
Sings his own praises
By speaking about his holy vows
And good works,
The adepts declare
That he is ignoble."

4. "*But the calm and contented monk,*
Who is not given to self-praise
By saying 'so I am' as regards his virtues,
Who is without any trace of haughtiness,
The adepts declare
That he is noble."

5. "*The one whose views are fabricated,*
False, prejudiced and impure
To the degree that he has a self-interest
In holding such views,
He would be basing himself on a peace
That is insecure."

6. "*Man shelters himself behind*
Philosophical dogmas.
After careful consideration,
He chooses one dogma
And rejects another.
Consequently, adopted dogmas
Are difficult to drop."

7. "*The pure person*
Has no views
Regarding different existences.
Having purified himself
Of deceit and conceit,
Where can he find any shelter?"

8. *"The person who has become*
Entangled in disputes
Is indeed entangled.
But how, and about what,
Could one dispute
With the independent person
Who has disentangled himself
From all disputes?
Concerning views,
He neither clings to,
Nor rejects them,
Having dropped them all."

17

Can Philosophy Purify Us?

That philosophy is not a help but a hindrance is the theme of the **Suddhatthakasutta**. There is the unmistakable suggestion that having no views is in fact the right view.

1. *"'Look! There is the pure person,*
Perfect and healthy, made pure
By means of the views he holds!'
Thinking in this way,
One falls back on knowledge,
Hoping thereby to find purity."

2. *"If a man's so-called purification*
Took place on account of his
Philosophical views,
Or if he rid himself of suffering
Because of that knowledge,
Then he is 'pure' while still retaining
His substrata!
Views are not the truth!"

3. *"But the Brahmin*
Who has detached himself
From what has been seen,

Heard or thought,
From virtue and good works
As well as good and evil,
Who has freed himself
From grasping
And whose actions are devoid
Of karmic consequences,
He does not say that
Purity comes from another."

4. *"By giving up a former view*
And opting for another,
They do not thereby cease
To cling.
Their ties are not broken.
They hold onto views
And then reject them,
Like a monkey that clutches
Onto one branch
And releases its grip on another."

5. *"The man who practises austerities,*
While being attached to
Sensory perception,
Goes in various directions.
But the sage,
Who has great wisdom
And understanding of the Dharma,
He does not go hither and thither."

6. *"He is free from*
All mental phenomena,
And from all that is seen,
Heard or thought.
So who in the world
Would entertain doubts about him,

Since he has deep insight
And moves about openly?"

7. "*Neither forming theories*
Nor having preferences,
He does not say,
'This is the pinnacle of purity'.
Having untied
The knot of attachment,
He never hankers after
Anything in the world."

8. "*The true Brahmin*
Transcends his limitations.
He does not hold
Onto anything
After knowing or seeing it.
Being free from both
Attachment and detachment,
He grasps at nothing."

18

The Wisdom of Having No Views

The **Paramatthakasutta** reiterates the importance of not getting involved in philosophical disputes, which are of no interest whatsoever to the Liberated.

1. *"When a self-opinionated person*
   Regards his views as
   'The highest' in the world
   In contrast to those of others
   That seem inferior to his,
   Such a person has failed
   To transcend disputes."

2. *"Clinging to whatever*
   He advantageously finds
   In what is seen, heard or thought,
   Or in virtue and good works,
   He rejects everything else
   With scorn."

3. *"The adepts call that view*
   A bond,
   For it acts as a base
   For viewing everything else

As inferior.
Therefore a monk must not depend
On what is seen, heard or thought,
Or upon virtue and good works."

4. *"Let him not form*
Any view in this world
On account of knowledge,
Virtue or good works.
He should never regard himself as
The equal of another,
Nor as being superior
Or inferior to another."

5. *"Giving up*
What had been grasped in the past,
And never again grasping,
He thereby ceases
To depend on anything,
Including dependence on knowledge.
When there are persons
With divergent ideas in a dispute,
He does not take sides.
He is free from views."

6. *"Having lost the desire*
To become this or become that,
Being free from wanting to exist
Either here or in the hereafter,
His mind does not escape into
Any doctrine,
For the mind is no longer given
To clinging."

7. *"Concerning things that have been*
Seen, heard or felt,
Not even any tiny thought

Does occur to him.
Who in the world can categorise
A Brahmin,
Who does not subscribe to
Any view whatsoever?"

8. "*Having neither views nor preferences,*
Being neither directed nor dominated
By doctrines,
The Brahmin is based
Neither on virtue nor good works.
As he has reached
The farther shore,
Such an individual
Never returns."

19

The Discourse on Decay

The title of this brief sutta, which is **Jarasutta,** is self-explanatory. The word "jara" means old age, decrepitude or decay. This term is closely related to "jaramaranam", which means old age and death.

Sooner or later every attachment of the mind brings us nothing but sorrow. Fully understanding our transitory nature results in the dropping of attachments, which is the state of detachment.

1. *"In truth, this life is short.*
   Within the span of a century
   We are no more.
   Should anyone live longer,
   He passes away
   Because of old age."

2. *"Springing from*
   Thoughts of 'mine'
   Man holds onto
   His cherished belongings
   That are all
   Never permanently his own.

Seeing that separation from them
Causes disappointment,
Why lead the life of a householder?"

3. *"Everything that man lays claim to,*
Saying 'this is mine',
He has to part from it at death.
Understanding this,
The wise devotee
Eschews egotism."

4. *"As an awakened sleeper*
Sees not the things
That came to pass during sleep,
So also one can never
See the dearest
Who are all dead
And gone forever."

5. *"When the names are mentioned*
Of those seen and heard,
Only their names will remain
Once they are dead."

6. *"The greedy in their egotism*
Fail to find freedom from suffering,
Lamentation and avarice.
Therefore, having given up greed,
And having seen the security
That is Nirvana,
The Munis (Sages) wander around."

7. *"For a solitary monk*
With a mind that is
Not tied to anything,
They say that it befits him
Never to reappear
In any form of existence."

8. *"The Sage, being detached*
In every situation,
Neither holding onto what is
Pleasant nor unpleasant,
Who is without greed,
Who no longer laments,
Is like the water
That sticks not
To a lotus leaf."

9. *"As a drop of water*
On a lotus leaf,
Or water on a lotus
Remains unsullied,
So is a Sage unsullied
By whatever that is seen,
Heard or thought."

10. *"The purified deem not*
That purity is obtainable
By means of what is seen,
Heard or thought,
Nor do they deem
That purity is obtainable
Through another,
They being neither satisfied
Nor dissatisfied
With anything."

20

Avoid Sexual Indulgence

Strong is the disapproval of sexual activity in the **Tissametteyyasutta.** The teachings of the Enlightened One in this regard are a far cry from those of cults that advocate sexual indulgence as a means to Enlightenment.

1. Tissa Metteyya: "O Venerable One, I like to know: What harm happens to a person who is given to sexual intercourse? After hearing your teachings, we shall practise them accordingly in seclusion."

2. *The Buddha: "Actually the teachings are lost*
On him who indulges in
Sexual intercourse.
He, in addition, follows
The wrong way.
It is not noble
Of him to do that."

3. *"When a man, having previously*
Wandered in solitude,
Lapses into lechery
In so far as
He has sexual intercourse,

He is like a derailed carriage.
In the world they call him
A low worldling."

4. *"His former fame and good name*
Is soon on the wane.
Let there be an ending
To sexual intercourse."

5. *"Overpowered by lustful thoughts,*
He is given to brooding
In the manner of a
Miserable person.
On hearing the
Disapproving words of others
He becomes unhappy."

6. *"Next he makes*
Weapons against himself
When reproached by others.
He degenerates
Into falsehood."

7. *"He is called 'wise'*
For starting to lead
A solitary life.
If later he leads a life
Of sexual indulgence instead,
He will have to face
The troubles of a fool."

8. *"Seeing this as suffering,*
Whether it happens earlier or later,
Let the Sage, remaining rooted
To his solitary life,
Never allow himself to be
Swayed by sexual intercourse."

9. *"Let him learn about*
The detachment of the mind,
Since this is best
For the noble life,
Without regarding himself
As being superior for that reason.
Such a person is surely near
To Nirvana."

10. *"The common people,*
Who are enslaved by carnal pleasures,
Are jealous of the
Sexuality-surpassed Sage,
Who has gone
Beyond the stream."

21

Desist from Debates

Often when a person argues with another about something, it is not so much a mutual and impartial investigation into a subject as an opportunity to promote certain preconceived ideas or beliefs. For some it is a chance to give full vent to their hidden anger, aggression or violence. Debates frequently become a means of showing off our clever intellects. It is beyond dispute that disputes provide us with a lot of excitement, entertainment and pleasure. Are we fully aware of the psychological reasons underlying the urge to argue? But those who are mindful or watchful of themselves will discover why they get a kick out of disputing.

When at Jetavana the Buddha preached the **Pasurasutta**, among those assembled there was a famous debater by the name of Pasura.

1. *"'This doctrine alone is pure',*
   They claim, thereby questioning
   The doctrines of others.
   Saying that what they are holding onto
   Is good,
   They become

Dogmatically entrenched
In the positions they have taken."

2. *"Craving for controversies,*
Plunging themselves into forums,
They regard each other
As foolish persons.
Presenting themselves
As experts in their fields,
And being eager for
The admiration of others,
They offer their debatable arguments."

3. *"Involved in disputatious discussions in public,*
And being hungry for praise,
They dread defeat.
But when others prove them wrong,
They become upset and
Resort to faultfinding."

4. *"The judges of the dispute*
Saw through his defective case
And declared that he was defeated.
'I have lost,' he said,
Crying out in grief."

5. *"Such verbal wars*
Have been fought between ascetics,
Resulting in the victors being
In high spirits
And the vanquished being
In low spirits.
Understanding this,
One desists from disputes,
For there is no advantage
In gaining fame
By means of disputation."

6. *"If he argues well and*
Settles the dispute before an assembly,
And for that reason
Wins praise,
He will feel very happy,
Having thus realised
His ambition."

7. *"That elated feeling*
Will cause him
Great suffering,
For he gives expression to
His pride.
Understanding this,
Desist from disputes,
For as the adepts say,
Purification cannot take place
By such means."

8. *"As a hero fed on royal food*
Seeks out an opponent,
In the same way,
O hero,
Seek your adversary
Wherever he might be,
Though no views are within you
For you to do any fighting
As in days of yore!"

9. *"If any persons, who,*
Having embraced philosophical views,
Were to claim that
'Only this is true',
Tell them that
'When a dispute arises
There will be no opposition

From the one
Without any views.'"

10. "*Concerning those*
Who wander about
And lead secluded lives,
Who never counter one view with another,
What opposition will you find
Among them,
O Pasura?
For them
Nothing that is grasped
Can be regarded as
The highest."

11. "*You came here thinking about*
Various views of a philosophical kind.
After meeting this purified person,
Proceeding with him will be
Impossible for you."

22

The Buddha Rejects a Proposal of Marriage

The **Magandiyasutta** is an account of the conversation between the Buddha and the wandering religious mendicant Magandiya.

Magandiya, the Brahmin, had a daughter of exceptional beauty. Although men of high standing were keen on marrying her, Magandiya did not think that any of them were deserving of this honour. He was evidently proud of his daughter's good looks while being a proud person himself.

Probably because of the Buddha's superhuman faculties, he was already aware that Magandiya and his wife would be receptive to his teachings. So when the Teacher visited their village he met Magandiya. After having noticed the auspicious marks on the Lord's body, Magandiya spoke to him about his daughter, and requested him to wait until her arrival. The Buddha remained silent. When Magandiya, accompanied by his wife and welldressed daughter appeared on the scene, they found the Muni missing!

Magandiya's wife, having found a footprint of the Buddha, and thereafter basing her judgement upon her arcane ability to read footprints, declared that the Buddha had totally transcended sensuality. Magandiya, however, ignoring his wife's statement, went ahead with his plan. Magandiya met the Buddha and offered him his daughter in marriage.

Would anybody who holds the Buddha in great reverence, either in ancient or modern times, have the audacity to put forward such a proposal? Was the Brahmin so ignorant that he did not know that the Sakyan Sage had already forsaken all worldly attachments? Was the man making a mockery of the Dharma, or trying hard to make the Enlightened One appear useless or foolish? Be that as it may, we can give Magandiya the benefit of the doubt. We can assume that he sincerely believed that only the Buddha was good enough to be his future son-in-law.

This sutta begins with the Master's comments on the matrimonial offer.

1. *The Buddha: "Even after seeing the*
Three daughters of Mara —
Tanha (Craving), Arati (Discontent)
And Raga (Lust),
There was not in me
The least desire for sexual intercourse!
What indeed is this,
Which is full of urine
And excreta?
I do not wish to touch her
Even with my foot!"

2. Magandiya: "If you do not like this treasure that is hungered after by many lords of men, what kind of view, good works, vows, way of life and becoming do you declare?"

3. *The Buddha: "Among the different views,*
I have not taken hold of any,
And then stated

'This do I declare'.
But, O Magandiya,
Having looked at the views,
Without grasping at any,
I found inner peace."

4. Magandiya: "You speak, O Sage, about all the views that have been formulated, without adopting any of them. As regards inner peace, how have the adepts described it?"

5. *The Buddha: "Not via view,*
Not by tradition,
Not by knowledge,
Not even by virtue and good works,
O Magandiya,
Does one come by
Complete cleansing.
Nor does one come by
Complete cleansing by
The absence of view,
Tradition, knowledge,
Virtue and good works.
Letting both the former
And the latter drop,
Without grasping,
Without any dependence,
The tranquil one is free
From becoming."

6. Magandiya: "If you maintain that complete cleansing comes from none of these, nor from the lack of them, your teaching is foolish indeed. Some believe that complete cleansing comes by means of view."

7. *The Buddha: "Relying upon views,*
O Magandiya,
You ask questions.

Because of what you have embraced,
You have no clarity.
You haven't the foggiest idea of
What I am saying.
Therefore it all seems foolish."

8. *"Whenever one regards oneself as*
Being the equal,
The superior or
The inferior of another,
Such a person is prone to disputing.
But whoever is free
From these three-fold
Forms of self-conceit,
He makes no such
Distinctions whatsoever."

9. *"As the genuine Brahmin*
Never distinguishes
Between what is 'equal' and
What is 'unequal',
Would he ever say 'this is true'
Or 'that is false'?"

10. *"Having left his home for good,*
The sage wanders homelessly,
Without forming friendships in a village,
Without indulging in sensual pleasures,
Without having any preferences and
Also without getting involved in
Disputes with people."

11. *"A great being*
Neither holds fast to those views
Nor disputes them,
Since these stand in the way of
Right conduct in the world.

As a lotus with a thorny stalk
Remains unspoilt
By mud and water,
So a sage,
An expounder of peace,
Being free from greed,
Remains unspoilt
By sensual pleasures and the world."

12. "*The adept*
Does not take pride in
View or thought,
For he is not of that kind.
Neither good works
Nor tradition guide him.
He does not take shelter in
The mental resting places
Of dogma."

13. "*Being detached*
As regards perception,
He is no longer
Tied to anything.
Being liberated
Through understanding,
He no longer has delusions.
But those who are attached to
Perceptions and views,
They wander about in the world
Creating conflict between people."

After they had heard and understood the Buddha's discourse, both Magandiya and his wife became Non-Returners (*Anagamins*). Non-Returners are never reborn in the world of men or of devas, but they go to the Pure Abodes (*Suddhavasa*) wherefrom they reach Nirvana.

It can be rightly argued that only those who have had first-hand or direct experience of that exalted and non-dualistic state of Nirvana are capable of making correct and reliable statements relating to it. This means that even after examining the question with an open and non-dogmatic mind, non-Arhats can never be absolutely sure about the nature of Nirvana.

The two contradictory statements in the 5th verse of this sutta might puzzle many a reader. This paradoxical verse with its opposing observations might at first glance seem impossible or unlikely, but still probably true on further reflection.

Verse 5 is as follows:

"Not via view,
Not by tradition,
Not by knowledge,
Not even by virtue and good works,
O Magandiya,
Does one come by
Complete cleansing.
Nor does one come by
Complete cleansing by
The absence of view,
Tradition, knowledge,
Virtue and good works.
Letting both the former
And the latter drop,
Without grasping,
Without any dependence,
The tranquil one is free
From becoming."

The foregoing bears a striking similarity to the following verse from the *Suddhatthakasutta*:

"The true Brahmin
Transcends his limitations.

He does not hold on
To anything
After knowing or seeing it.
Being free from both
Attachment and detachment,
He grasps at nothing."

To paraphrase the Buddha's advice to Magandiya:

By following various methods one does not come by complete cleansing. Nor does one come by complete cleansing by not following various methods.

Expressed differently, by means of effort one cannot find Liberation: nor can one find it without effort.

The following statement is open to interpretation:

"Being free from both
Attachment and detachment,
He grasps at nothing."

Let us now examine what happens to the mind after reading these verses and reflecting on them:

1. One hears or reads about the truth that freedom from attachment is necessary in order to find Liberation.
2. Then without fully understanding that truth, without getting to the heart of the matter, the mind reduces the truth to a mere *idea* : the idea that freedom from attachment is necessary to find Liberation. Since the mind cannot survive without ideas, it is not difficult to see why the mind has this craving for ideas. Given that the mind gets its intellectual nourishment from ideas, it is not surprising that it reduces even the Dharma to nothing but a bundle of ideas. Therefore we get attached to the *idea* that freedom from attachment is indispensable for attaining Nirvana.
3. Next, feeling uneasy about the aforementioned attachment: namely, the attachment to the *idea* that freedom from

attachment is indispensable for attaining Nirvana, seeing the danger of retaining even this attachment, regarding every attachment as an obstacle to that ultimate Release, what does the mind do? The mind reacts to this situation by inventing the new *idea* that freedom from this attachment to the *idea* of detachment is a requirement for Liberation.

4. How the mind likes to look at Nirvana from one standpoint now and from another standpoint later! Why do we everlastingly dwell in the valley of suffering with our various views failing to vanish?
5. Grasping at nothing, having no views whatsoever, the view-making machinery stops. Being fully free from both attachment and detachment, and thereby transcending the opposites, one comes by that Tranquility, which is causeless.

23

The Inner Calmness of the Supreme Sage

The Buddha's short sermon on the various distinguishing qualities of the calmed sage is recorded in the **Purabhedasutta**:

1. Questioner: "What insight and what virtue make a person of inner peace? Tell me, O Gotama, about that supreme sage."

2. *The Buddha: "His cravings ceased*
Even before the ending
Of his body.
His past has died out.
He does not concern himself
With what is current.
He has no preferences whatsoever
Regarding the future."

3. *"In him there is no anger,*
No fear, no boasting
And no misbehaviour.
Speaking wisely
And not puffed up,

He is indeed a sage
Of quiet and controlled words."

4. "*Neither clinging onto the future*
Nor lamenting the past,
Remaining unspoilt
By sense impressions,
He is not misled
By any view."

5. "*He is unattached.*
He is free from deceit,
Covetousness, avarice
And obtrusiveness.
Neither is he objectionable
Nor is he a slanderer."

6. "*Neither does he feel drawn to*
What is pleasant
Nor is he proud.
Gentle and quick-witted,
He is neither credulous
Nor repelled by anything."

7. "*It is not to obtain anything*
That he learns and trains himself,
And if nothing is gained,
He is not distressed.
Remaining untouched by craving,
He hungers not
For what is sweet."

8. "*With equanimity*
(Evenness of mind or temper),
Or Upekkha (indifference
To pain and pleasure),
He is constantly mindful or watchful.
Not regarding anyone in the world

As his equal,
Nor as his superior,
Nor as his inferior,
He has no desire
For self-elevation."

9. "*Having understood the Dharma,*
He is entirely independent
In the sense that he does not depend
On anything.
In him there cannot be found
Any longing for existence
Nor non-existence."

10. "*Him do I call 'calmed',*
Who loses interest in sensual pleasures,
Breaks all bonds
And ceases to cling."

11. "*For he is without sons,*
Cattle, fields or wealth.
He grasps at nothing.
He rejects nothing."

12. "*Unaffected by the accusations made*
Against him by ordinary people,
Including ascetics and Brahmins,
He remains unruffled
By their words."

13. "*Letting go of greed,*
The sage does not categorise himself as
Being 'superior',
'Inferior' or 'equal'.
With a mind that no longer measures,
He attains the timeless
And immeasurable."

14. "*Owning nothing in the world,*

Neither sorrowing over the loss
Of anything that no longer exists
Nor walking into the trap of
Mental phenomena,
He has indeed attained
Inward quietude."

24

What Makes Us Quarrel?

What is the origin of disputes? The **Kalahavivada Sutta** deals with this subject. The Buddha preached this sermon in a place close to his famous birthplace at Kapilavatthu. After listening to this discourse, the Buddha's foster mother, Maha Pajapati Gotami, decided to renounce the world.

1. Questioner: "What is the origin of contentions, disputes, lamentations, sorrows, selfishness, conceit, arrogance and slander? From where do these come? Please tell me this."

2. *The Buddha: "From that which has become dear*
There will arise contentions, disputes,
Lamentations, sorrows,
Selfishness, conceit,
Arrogance and slander.
Contentions and disputes
Are connected with selfishness.
Contention gives birth to slander."

3. Questioner: "What is the origin of things that are dear in the world, along with greed that is found in the world? What is the origin of man's hopes for the afterlife and the fulfilments thereof?"

4. *The Buddha: "It is desire*
That is the cause of things
That are dear in the world,
Along with greed
That is found in the world.
It is also the cause of
Man's hopes for the afterlife and
The fulfilments thereof."

5. Questioner: "From where does desire originate in the world? Wherefrom do the following originate: judgements, anger, falsehood, doubt and other predispositions pointed out by the Ascetic Gotama?"

6. *The Buddha: "In the world people see things as*
'This is pleasant' or
'That is unpleasant'.
That way of viewing is
The origin of desire.
The judgements that
Men make in the world
Are based on their seeing
The appearing and disappearing
Of physical things."

7. *"The states of anger,*
Falsehood and doubt arise
Because of this duality —
'Pleasant' and 'unpleasant'.
Let a doubter learn about
The path of knowledge
In order to understand these states
As shown by the Ascetic."

8. Questioner: "Why not go into the whys and wherefores of regarding things as 'pleasant' or 'unpleasant'? What must be removed so that these states are no longer present?

Regarding the appearing and disappearing of things, how does this phenomenon originate?"

9. *The Buddha: "'Sense-impression'*
Is the cause of
'What is pleasant' or
'What is unpleasant'.
These two states
Will be absent
When sense-impression
Is also absent.
This, I say, is also the cause of
The phenomenon of
Appearing and disappearing of things."

10. Questioner: "From what does sense-experience originate? From what does grasping begin? With the disappearance of what does grasping end? With the disappearance of what will sense-impression end?"

11. *The Buddha: "Sense-impressions get distorted*
When the mind is conditioned
By name-and form (the past).
Grasping has its origin
In desire.
When desire ends,
Thoughts of 'mine'
No longer exist.
When one is no longer conditioned
By name-and-form (the past),
The distorting
Of sense impressions ends."

12. Questioner: "What is the stage of a person for whom form has disappeared? Also, how do pleasure and pain cease to exist? Tell me how it ends, because my mind is keen to understand this."

13. *The Buddha: "Neither is his perception normal*
Nor is it abnormal (deranged).
Besides, he is not
Without perception,
Nor does he perceive
What has gone (the past).
For one who achieves this state,
Form disappears,
Because his perception
Originates in understanding
The diffuseness
Of the phenomenal world."

14. Questioner: "You have answered all our questions. Now we ask you another one. Do answer the following question as well. Do not some of the self-styled wise persons proclaim that the supreme purity is to this extent, or do they maintain that it is something else?"

15. *The Buddha: "Indeed, some say that*
The supreme purity is to this extent,
Yet some self-styled experts maintain
The doctrine of annihilation wherein
No grasping whatsoever will remain."

16. *"Understanding that they*
Are all dependent on theories,
Seeing that on which they rely,
The Sage
Does not get involved in disputes.
The Muni in his wisdom
Is free
From the chain of repeated existence."

25

There is Only One Truth

Many are the disagreements among philosophers. Clashes between them are frequent. They hold and express contradictory views. In the **Culaviyuhasutta** the Buddha shows that although they propound different truths, actually there is only one truth. Because of the discordant views of philosophers, the world is in a state of conflict.

1. Questioner: "Some quarrelsome experts with firmly-held views assert themselves by making various statements. They say: 'Whoever holds these views understands the Dharma. Whoever repudiates them is not perfect.'"

2. "After entering a contest, they argue that their 'opponent is foolish and ignorant'. When they all claim to be experts, which theory of theirs is an expression of the truth?"

3. *The Buddha: "When one person brands*
His opponent
As a fool, a beast,
Or an extremely dim-witted man
Merely because of
Differences of opinion between them,
Then **all** *indeed are fools, beasts*

And extremely dim-witted,
Since they all have
Their own views."

4. *"If each person*
Could purify himself
By means of his views,
He would be of
Pure understanding,
Skilled and wise!
None with dogmatic views
Would be stupid!"

5. *"I do* **not** *say*
'This is the truth',
Which is something that
Fools do between themselves.
Since they regard
Their own dogmatic views as
The truth,
They treat others as fools."

6. Questioner: "What some declare to be true, others say it is untrue. Thus they tenaciously cling to their views. Why do ascetics fail to say one and the same thing?"

7. *The Buddha: "There is but one truth:*
There is not a second,
About which the intelligent
Would quarrel between themselves.
Since ascetics express different truths,
They of course do not speak
With one accord."

8. Questioner: "Why do these self-styled experts express different truths? Is there a wide range of truths or do they indulge in conjectural thinking?"

9. *The Buddha: "There is not*
A wide range of eternal truths
In the world,
Except for their misperceptions.
But based on their speculative
Justification of their views,
They distinguish between
Truth and falsehood."

10. *"Relying upon what is seen, heard,*
Ascetic disciplines, religious vows or thought,
He becomes contemptuous
Of others.
Resolute and self-satisfied,
He declares that his rivals are
Not adepts but fools."

11. *"Since he considers his opponents fools,*
He regards himself as an expert.
Having styled himself 'expert',
He pours scorn on the others
And speaks in this vein."

12. *"Overflowing with views,*
Feeling proud of himself,
Suffering from the delusion of
Being perfect,
He then uses his mind
To sanctify not only himself
But also his opinions."

13. *"If an opponent imputes inferiority,*
Thus making a person believe
That he is for that reason 'inferior',
Then the opponent, along with that person,
Is of inferior intelligence.
When, by the same token, he imagines

That he is Enlightened,
Then among the ascetics there will soon be
None who is a fool!"

14\. "*'Those who expound any teaching*
Other than this
Are wanting in purity,
Hence they are imperfect,'
Declare the heretical gurus individually.
Such is their deep emotional commitment to
Their own doctrines."

15\. "*'Here only are the teachings pure,*
For other doctrines are devoid of purity,'
Insist the heretical gurus,
Each remaining loyal to
His own particular school of thought."

16\. "*When speaking strongly about*
His own school of thought,
Whom else but himself
Should he treat
As a fool?
For he only brings conflict
On himself
When he accuses his opponent
Of foolishness and
Of subscribing to an impure doctrine."

17\. "*Taking a position,*
Using oneself as a yardstick for measuring,
He enters the arena of controversy!
But the person
Who simply gives up
All decision-making
Never becomes a troublemaker
In the world."

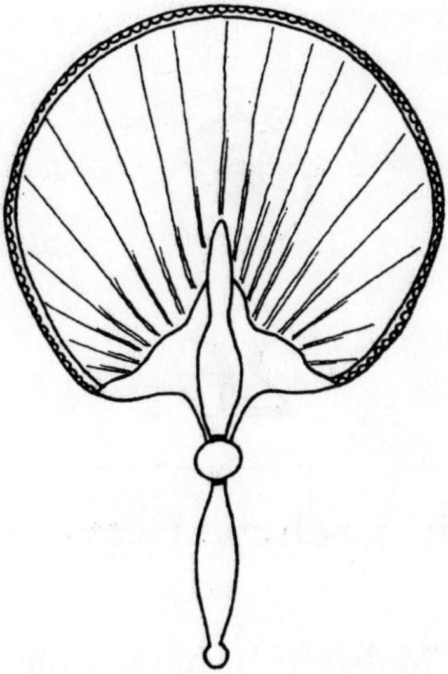

26

Munis Eschew Every View

Central to the **Mahaviyuhasutta** is the great truth that perfect purity becomes possible only by divesting oneself of views. Variously described as views, speculative ideas, theories, doctrines, dogmas or teachings, this sutta shows the importance of not getting oneself imprisoned in any of these mind-made prison cells, so to speak.

1. Questioner: "There are those who adhere to their philosophical views. 'This alone is the truth,' they assert during debates. Do they deserve blame, or are they worthy of praise?"

2. *The Buddha: "Yes, but it is a trivial thing*
   That is insufficient
   To attain tranquillity.
   Debates bear two fruits:
   Seeing this truth,
   One avoids disputes;
   And seeing that state of security,
   Let none engage in disputes."

3. *"The wise one,*
   Being free,

Distances himself
From the views held by people.
How could he,
Who is free from entanglements,
Become entangled,
As he is already free
From what has been seen and heard?"

4. *"Regarding ascetic practices*
As uppermost,
Some say that purity is attainable
By means of self-restraint.
So they begin a practice
And strictly adhere to it,
Saying 'only by training ourselves in this
We will become pure'.
Despite their claim to be experts,
They are guided
To becoming."

5. *"Should anyone not keep*
The vows he has made
Or should fail
To follow his precepts,
He will tremble
With a sense of failure.
He will lament and long for
Purity in this world,
Like the person
Who has lost his caravan
And is far away from home."

6. *"But the one who renounces*
All ascetic practices,
Including vows and all activities,
Be these blameful

Or blameless,
Who desires neither purity
Nor impurity,
He is a detached wanderer
Who promotes peace."

7. *"By means of austerities,*
Or anything disliked,
Or what has been seen
Or heard, or thought,
They talk about purity
While moving upwards,
Without letting go
Of their craving for
One rebirth after another."

8. *"One with desires*
Is given to having longings,
And he trembles about his
Preconceived views.
But when for a person
There is no death
And subsequent birth,
How can he be given to trembling
Or desiring?"

9. Questioner: "Some describe the doctrine as the highest, whereas others describe it as the lowest. Which description is correct, for each describer is a self-styled expert?"

10. "They dispute, each ascribes superiority to his own doctrines and inferiority to those of others. Each asserts that his doctrines alone are the truth."

11. *The Buddha: "If a teaching becomes inferior*
Merely because an opponent
Disapproves of it,
Then none of the teachings

Would stand out as being the best.
For many speak disparagingly
Of the teachings of others
But praise their own to the skies."

12. *"The adoration of their doctrines*
Is to the same extent as their praise
Of their own private paths.
All doctrines would therefore be 'true',
For their so-called purity
Is exclusively theirs!"

13. *"There is nothing*
That a Brahmin needs
From another person.
After examining the doctrines,
There is nothing
That he would want to take
From any of them.
Therefore having gone beyond
The field of controversy,
He does not regard
Any other Dharma
As being the best."

14. *"Believing that purity can be attained*
By means of view,
Some say 'I know. I see,
This is actually so!'
If they had truly seen it,
What is its use to them?
For they, having violated
The noble path,
Declare that purity is attainable by
Other means!"

15. *"The insightful*
See name-and-form,
And having seen,
They will understand only that.
But regardless of whether
The insightful
See much or little,
The 'experts' say that no cleansing
Will take place by such means."

16. *"By means of his preconceived views*
No dogmatist can ever reach
That purified realm.
Maintaining that his views have merit,
He talks about purity and
His realisation of it."

17. *"No genuine Brahmin finds freedom*
By means of the inventions
Of the imagination.
Neither is he a view-follower
Nor a knowledge-gatherer.
Despite his awareness
Of people's varied views,
These remain a matter
Of total indifference to him."

18. *"The Sage,*
Having disentangled himself
From the knots in the world,
Is never a party to a dispute.
Calm among the agitated,
This equanimous person
Does not accept views,
While others seize them."

19. *"Having dropped*
His old Asavas (cankers),
And by not creating any new ones,
The desireless person
No longer hankers after views.
Fully free is he from every view.
Neither is he attracted
By the world that he views
Nor does he view
Himself disapprovingly."

20. *"He has ceased having*
Any connection
With mental phenomena:
Whatever has been seen,
Heard or thought.
In so far as all these links
Have been broken,
The Sage has totally
Unburdened himself
And is completely liberated.
He does not fall into any category.
Gone beyond
The confines of time,
There is neither abstaining
Nor desiring."
"Let him put an end
To the delusion of
'I am'.
By means of mindfulness
He learns about
All his cravings
That arise within,
And they are dispelled."

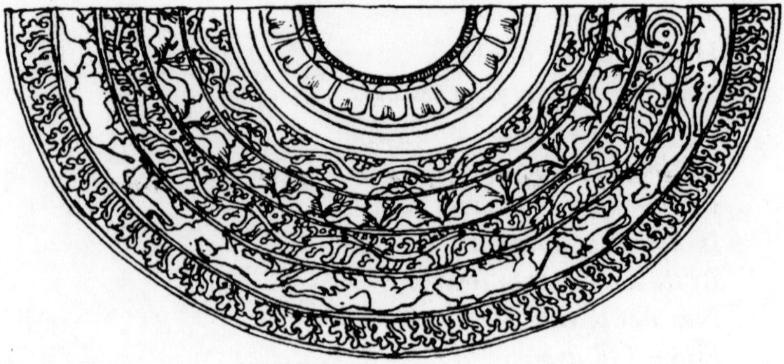

27

O Bhikkhus, Briskly Break Your Bonds

Although the **Tuvatakasutta** (*Sutta on Hurrying Up*) is mostly about the dos and don'ts that monks must always bear in mind, the advice and hints stated herein are of inestimable value to laypersons with a serious interest in the Dharma.

1. Questioner: "I request you, Great Sage and Kinsman of the Sun, to speak about seclusion and the serene state. Once the monk has understanding, in what manner does he become calmed and unattached to anything of this world?"

2. *The Buddha: "Let him put an end*
   To the delusion of
   'I am'.
   By means of mindfulness
   He learns about
   All his cravings
   That arise within,
   And they are dispelled."

3. *"Let him come to know*
   Every truth
   From either within himself

Or outside,
But let him not become
Firmly established in any,
For the good
Do not call that 'calmed'."

4. *"Let him not for that reason*
Regard himself as
Being better
Or lower than others,
Or equal to them.
Let him not,
Having had diverse forms of contact,
Start creating mental images
Relating to himself
That result in the 'self'."

5. *"Let the monk,*
Having discovered
That inward calm,
Never seek it from
An outward source.
Since he has not grasped
At anything,
Is there anything
Left to reject?"

6. *"As the waveless stillness*
Of the mid-ocean,
So must be the stillness
Of the monk.
Remaining unruffled,
Let him not desire
Anything whatsoever."

7. Questioner: "O Open-Eyed One, who has explained to me the danger-dispelling Dharma that you have personally

discovered, now do talk about religious practices, disciplinary rules and concentration (*Samadhi*)."

8. *The Buddha: "Let not a monk have*
Greedy eyes.
Let him turn a deaf ear
To town-talk.
Let him not hanker after
Delicious dishes.
Let him not cling to
Any mundane thing."

9. *"Whenever a monk is affected*
By disagreeable contact,
Let him not be given to grieving.
Neither does he yearn for
Existence anywhere
Nor does danger
Give him a fright."

10. *"Let him not store up boiled rice,*
Food, drink and cloth,
And let him not be afraid
Should he receive nothing."

11. *"Let him meditate,*
Not idly roam around.
Let him not behave badly
Nor be heedless.
Let him live in a noiseless abode
With seats and couches."

12. *"Let him not oversleep,*
But let him devote himself to
Being wakeful — watchfulness.
Let him give up laziness,
Deceit, laughter, sport,

Sexual intercourse and everything
Associated with it."

13. *"Let him not practise Atharva charms*
Nor interpret physical marks,
Dreams and stars (astrology).
Let not my followers make predictions
Based on animal cries
Nor should they practise healing
And the art of impregnating."

14. *"Let him not become crest-fallen*
When others criticise him.
Let him not become swollen-headed
When others pay him compliments.
Let him throw aside greed,
Avarice, anger and slander."

15. *"Let a monk neither buy nor sell.*
Let him not do anything anywhere
For which he will have to take the blame.
Let him not linger in villages.
Let him not talk to people
With the intention
Of gaining anything."

16. *"Let not a bhikkhu become a boaster,*
Nor should he speak
With ulterior motives.
Let him not be insolent
Nor say things that end in
Disputatious discord."

17. *"Let him not allow himself*
To be misled
By listening to lies.
Let him never act
Out of malice.

Let him not dislike anyone
On account of his manner
Of living, understanding,
Vows or virtues."

18. "*Let him not,*
After hearing the upsetting words
Of talkative ascetics and ordinary folk,
Retort angrily with severe sentences,
Since the calmed
Do not speak likewise
In reprisal."

19. "*Let the searchful*
And ever-watchful monk,
Having understood
The foregoing Dharma,
Abide by it.
Realising that the purified realm
Is none other
Than serenity,
He remains attentive
To what Gotama taught."

20. "*Let the monk be*
Ever watchful
Let him pay homage
To the Exalted One,
The Unsurpassed Surpasser,
Who with his own eyes
Saw the Dharma
Instead of basing his knowledge
On mere hearsay."

28

Special Qualities of the Munis

The **Attadandasutta** recommends courses of action that are indispensable for realising that final Release.

The "arrow stuck in the heart" is probably a metaphor for the arrow of greed (*Lobha*), hatred (*Dosa)* and delusion (*Moha*). These three unwholesome conditions, when considered together, are like a piercing arrow that causes perpetual pains and problems.

1. *The Buddha: "The prevalence of violence*
   Is the cause of fear.
   See how people quarrel!
   I will recall my experience of it."

2. *"When I saw people*
   Engaged in a struggle,
   Like struggling fish
   In meagre water,
   I was filled with fear."

3. *"The world everywhere*
   Is without substance
   And insecure.
   Every direction
   Is in a state of flux.

I wanted for myself
A house of safety
But failed to find any
That is free."

4. *"Much to my disgust I realised*
That there is nothing in the end
But strife.
Then I noticed something
That is so difficult to see —
An arrow stuck in the heart."

5. *"Pierced by this arrow,*
The victim runs hither and thither.
Once the arrow
Is pulled out,
Neither does one run
Nor sink."

6. *"Concerning worldly fetters,*
Be free from them!
Understanding the nature
Of sensual pleasures,
Do drop them,
And prepare yourself
Along the path
To Nirvana!"

7. *"Be truthful!*
Be free from impudence,
Deceit, anger and slander!
Thus the sage
Goes beyond greed."

8. *"The man whose mind*
Is Nirvana-orientated
Casts aside drowsiness, laziness
And lethargic indifference.

Let him neither indolent
Nor arrogant be."

9. *"Let him not lapse*
Into lying
Nor become attached
To sense objects
Or forms.
Let him purge himself
Of pride.
Let him ensure
That his violence
Vanishes without trace."

10. *"Let him not be glad*
Of what is old
Nor develop a liking
For what is new.
Let him not be sad
About what is lost,
Nor cling to
What is pleasant."

11. *"Greed, I declare,*
Is the great flood.
Hankering is
The quick current.
Getting fixed in desire is
The base of the stream.
Getting out
Of the morass of sensuality
Is difficult."

12. *"Never turning traitor*
To the truth,
The sage, the Brahmin,
Stands on solid ground.

As he has detached himself
From all and everything,
He indeed
Can be called 'calmed'."

13. "*Having personally discovered*
And realised the Dharma,
He is not dependent
On anything.
Correctly does he
Conduct himself in the world
Without being jealous of anyone."

14. "*He who has transcended sensuality,*
This chain that is so difficult
To unchain,
Is not given
To sorrowing or worrying.
For he has gone
Beyond the stream
And is free from ties."

15. "*Let your past wither away;*
Let there be nothing left
For the future.
If in between,
Which is the present,
There is no clinging,
Then calmed will you be
While wandering."

16. "*The person who*
As regards his
Entire psychophysical entity
Is totally devoid
Of any sense of 'me',
And who for that reason

Never sorrows
Over what in fact does not exist,
Has no sense of loss in the world."

17. "*Self-centred thoughts such as*
'This is mine' or 'this is theirs'
Do not occur to him.
Being free
From acquisitiveness,
Seeing that
Nothing really belongs to him,
He never complains 'I don't have this'."

18. "*Those who are not given*
To fearful trembling
Have certain advantages.
They are free
From harshness,
Greed and desire.
They, in addition,
Remain undisturbed
In every situation."

19. "*The man who*
Ceases to crave,
Who understands,
Gathers neither merit
Nor demerit.
As he no longer
Accumulates anything,
He discovers
Happiness everywhere."

20. "*The Muni* (Sage)
Does not identify himself
As being one among equals,
Inferiors or superiors.

Being calm
And craving-free,
He neither accepts nor rejects."

29

Guidelines for Leading the Pure Life

As the life of a monk is fraught with many frustrations, difficulties and problems, Sariputta put questions to the Master about these matters. Sariputta was the foremost among the monks. In the **Sariputtasutta** the Buddha set forth his guidelines for leading the pure life, which is the prelude to Enlightenment. The Buddha's invaluable advice on that occasion can be followed not only by monks and nuns, but laypersons as well.

1. Sariputta: "Never before have I seen nor have I heard from any person about such a sweet-voiced Teacher, who with his entourage has come down from the celestial abode of Tusita."
2. "As he, the Clear-Sighted One, who manifests himself in the world of gods and men, driving out the darkness of ignorance, having attained bliss single-handedly."
3. "To this Awakened One, who is independent, resolute and free from deception, I have come with a question that I ask on behalf of the many here who are not free from fetters."

4. "For an unhappy monk, who resorts to a secluded site, such as the foot of a tree, a cemetery or a mountain cave,"

5. "Or different kinds of beds, what dangers lurk there for him which should not make him tremble, while still dwelling in quiet surroundings?"

6. "How many earthly dangers will the monk have to face when going to the deathless region, which he must overcome in his secluded setting?"

7. "What should be his manner of speaking?
   What deeds should he do?
   What should a steadfast monk's precepts and practices be?"

8. "By undertaking what, having one-pointedness of mind, intelligence and attentiveness, can he purify himself from his own filth, as a silversmith frees the silver from its dross?"

9. *The Buddha: "O Sariputta,*
   I will explain to you,
   Since I do understand it,
   What would be pleasant for him
   Who is fed up with the world,
   If he stays in a lonely place
   And aspires after Enlightenment
   In conformity with the Dharma."

10. "*Let the mindful monk,*
    Exercising self-restraint,
    Never harbour
    The following five fears:
    The fear of stinging insects,
    Swooping flies, snakes,
    Human contact
    And four-footed animals."

11. "*Let him not fear
The followers of other teachings,
Even after observing
The many hazards therein.
Besides, while aspiring
After the good,
He must surmount
All other perils.*"

12. "*Suffering from disease
And with hunger pangs,
Let him endure
Both cold and extreme heat;
And being affected by them
In many ways,
And being homeless,
He should work hard persistently.*"

13. "*Let him not steal
And let him not tell a lie;
Let him treat with loving-kindness
Both the weak and the strong.
Whenever his mind is
In a disturbed state,
Being well aware of it,
He just drops the disturbance,
Regarding it as
A friend of Mara (the Dark One).*"

14. "*Let him not come under the control
Of anger or arrogance.
Having rooted these out,
He remains steady.
He bears without resistance
Both the pleasant
And the unpleasant.*"

15. *"Giving priority to wisdom,*
Taking delight in what is good,
He should discard those dangers.
Let him drop his discontent
In his secluded dwelling;
He must give up
Having the following four
Grief-stricken thoughts:"

16. *"'What shall I eat?'*
'Where shall I eat?'
'How badly I slept!'
'Where shall I sleep tonight?'
Let the homeless wanderer
Go beyond such thoughts."

17. *"Having at the right time*
Been the recipient of food and cloth,
He should know that
Moderation results in joy.
Guarded, he behaves
With restraint in the village,
Where he avoids harsh speech
Even under provocation."

18. *"With downcast eyes,*
Without being given to loafing around,
He is keen on meditation
And extremely wakeful.
Having attained equanimity,
Let him with a calm mind
Bring to an end
All room for doubt
And all misconduct."

19. *"When assailed with words of blame,*
He should be glad

And remain mindful.
He should treat his fellow-seekers
With open-heartedness.
Let him give expression
To good words at the right time.
Let him turn his mind away
From people's talk and gossip."

20. "*There are, besides,*
Five kinds of taints in the world,
Wherefrom he must extricate himself
By means of mindfulness —
The cravings for forms,
Sounds, tastes, smells
And tactile sensations."

21. "*When the mindful monk*
Drops his desire
For these things,
Dwells on the Dharma
In due season
And is undeviatingly devoted
To watchfulness,
His state of darkness disappears."

30

The Head and its Splitting

Very deep insights into the Dharma become particularly evident as the *Sutta-Nipata* unfolds and draws to an end. Its concluding chapters concern themselves with the Path to the Beyond. The opening verses of the **Vatthugatha** are about the sufferings of Bavari as the consequence of a life-threatening curse. Knowing this historical background might be helpful to understand and appreciate the suttas fully. With the assistance of such contextual information our comprehension of the discourses and dialogues can become deeper. Moreover, contemplating these texts over and over again not only makes us increasingly aware of the timeless qualities and profundities therein but also reinforces our devotion to the Dharma.

In a hermitage situated on the banks of the Godhavari River in central India there lived a Brahmanical ascetic by the name of Bavari. Having received the revenue of a neighbouring village, Bavari extravagantly spent all his money on a great sacrifice. Consequently, the man was in reduced circumstances. On one occasion a fellow Brahmin visited Bavari and demanded five hundred pieces of money. Bavari responded that he was poverty-stricken. Thereupon the visitor angrily cursed him.

"Seven days from today," said the visiting Brahmin, "may your head split up into seven pieces!"

Bavari became very disturbed in mind. But a celestial being (*Devata*), who had been Bavari's mother in a previous existence, realised that Bavari was in a difficult situation. Therefore the celestial being, who was desirous of restoring Bavari's self-confidence and composure, informed him that the Brahmin who had demanded the money did not know the meaning of "head" or "the splitting of it".

"In that case, who knows it?" remarked Bavari.

The celestial being informed him of the living presence in the world of the Enlightened One.

Was the celestial being subtly suggesting that "the splitting" of the head, metaphorically speaking, referred to the inward purification of the mind and the consequent discarding of its sinister traits?

Following the celestial being's advice, Bavari immediately sent his sixteen disciples to the Buddha. Each of them asked him a question. The Lord's masterly replies to those questions are among the most treasured sayings in Buddhist literature.

1. With the intention of attaining the state of nothingness, a Brahmin who was well versed in the hymns, left the lovely city of the Kosalas and moved southwards.
2. He lived on the banks of the Godhavari River in Assaka, near Alaka, where he subsisted on gatherings and fruit.
3. The close-by village was large. He used the money he received from that village to perform a great sacrifice.
4. Thereafter he entered the hermitage. No sooner had he entered than another Brahmin arrived,
5. With swollen feet, thirst, stained teeth and a dusty head. He approached Bavari and demanded five hundred pieces of money.

6. Bavari received him, offered him a seat, enquired after his health and well being, and started speaking.
7. Bavari: "I have parted with all the gifts I once had. Excuse me, O Brahmin, but I do not have five hundred pieces."
8. The Brahmin: "If you do not give me what I ask, may your head split up into seven pieces seven days from now."
9. The deceitful man uttered a curse. After hearing his words Bavari was filled with sorrow.
10. Grief-stricken, he avoided taking any food. Such was his mental state that meditation was no longer a source of joy.
11. Noticing his fearful and miserable condition, a well-intended deity approached Bavari and spoke as follows:
12. The deity: "That deceiver, who craves riches, knows nothing about the head nor its splitting."
13. Bavari: "Then, if you know it, tell me about the head and its splitting. I am keen to know."
14. The deity: "I, too, do not know this; knowledge about this I do not have. As regards heads and head-splitting, that really is the vision of the Conquerors."
15. Bavari: "Who then within the earth's great confines knows about the head and its splitting? Do tell me, O deity."
16. The deity: "From the city of Kapilavatthu the world leader has gone forth. He is the Sakyan scion of King Okkaka. He is the torchbearer of humanity."
17. "He, O Brahmin, is certainly the All-Awakened One. Not only has he gone to the farther shore of all phenomena but has also gained all higher knowledge and the powers. He has insight into all phenomena. He has transcended all traits. Having abandoned the substrata of existence, he is fully liberated."

18. "He is the Buddha, the Venerable or Worshipful One in the world. Having supernatural insight, he expounds the Dharma. Go to him and ask, for he will clarify it for you."

19. On hearing the word "*Sambuddho*" (Fully-Awakened) Bavari became elated and his sorrow somewhat subsided. He experienced a strong fit of rapture.

20. Ecstatic, exhilarated and excited, Bavari made a request:

    Bavari: "In which village, town or country does the Saviour of the World dwell, so that we can visit him and pay homage to the Fully-Awakened One, the Foremost of Men?"

21. The deity: "At Savatthi in Kosala does he dwell. This very wise Conqueror of superior intelligence is an unexcelled Sakyan, who is fully free and cankerless. This chief of men knows well the art of head-splitting."

11. Then he spoke with his pupils, those mantra-mastered Brahmins.

    Bavari: "Come, young Brahmins, I am going to speak. Listen!"

12. "Rarely does such a being appear on earth. Right now he is in the world. He is widely renowned as the All-Enlightened (*Sambuddho*). Hasten to Savatthi and see the greatest of men!"

24. The Brahmins: "When we see him, O Brahmin, how are we to know that he is in fact the Buddha? Explain this to us for we are in the dark!"

25. Bavari: "The signs of a Superman have all been handed down in our hymns, and there are thirty-two signs in number."

26. "Whenever these marks manifest themselves in such a man's limbs, there are only two courses of action open to him: a third course of action does not exist."

27. "If he were to lead the life of a householder, he would become the sovereign ruler of the entire earth, ruling it non-violently without cudgel or sword, but in accordance with Dharma."
28. "But if he forsakes hearth and home and gives preference to the homeless life, he will become the remover of the world's veil, the incomparable Fully-Awakened Arhat."
29. "Pose questions mentally concerning my birth and clan, my marks, the mantras that I know, my pupils and also the head and its splitting."
30. "If he is the clear-sighted Buddha, then he will answer by word of mouth the questions that you will have only made mentally."
31. Ater hearing Bavari's words, his sixteen Brahmanic pupils — Ajita, Tissametteyya, Punnaka, and Mettagu,
32. Dhotaka, Upasiva, Nanda, Hemaka, Todeyya, Kappa and the wise Jatukanni,
33. Bhadravudha, Udaya, Posala, the intelligent Mogharaja and the great sage Pingiya —
34. Each being the chief of a group of pupils; all being world famous and devoted to meditative absorptions; having in their minds the impressions of their past lives —
35. With matted hair and dressed in deer skins, respectfully saluted Bavari by going round him towards the right, and set out northwards thereafter.
36. They went to Patitthana of Alaka, then to Mahissati, and also to Ujjeni, Gonaddha, Vedisa, Vanasa,
37. To Kosambi, Saketa, Savatthi which is the best of cities, Setavya, Kapilavatthu and to Kusinara,
38. To Pava, which is the city of riches, to Vesali, which is the city of the Magadhans, and to the delightful and beautiful shrine Pasanaka.

39. As a thirsty man is eager for cool water, as a merchant is eager to amass a fortune, or as a sunburned man is eager for shade, so did they hastily climb the mountain.
40. At that time the Buddha was preaching the Dharma before an assembly of monks. It was like the roaring of a lion in the forest.
41. Ajita saw the Fully-Awakened One, who seemed like the rayless shining sun, or the full moon on the fifteenth night.
42. Having noticed all the Lord's bodily marks, he was absolutely delighted. He stood aside and mentally framed these questions:
43. Ajita: "Do speak about my master's birth, clan, and marks, including his mastery of the hymns. How many of them can the Brahmin recite?"
44. *The Buddha: "One hundred and twenty years*
Is his age;
He is a Bavari
With three marks on his body.
As regards the three Vedas,
He has mastered them."
45. "*Well versed in the marks,*
Legends, etymologies and rituals,
He is the teacher of five hundred persons.
Concerning his own teachings,
He has attained the highest."
46. Ajita: "O Highest of Humans, who let go of craving, describe Bavari's marks so that we have no misgivings about him."
47. *The Buddha: "With his tongue*
He can cover his face;
There is hair between his eyebrows
And his male organ is sheathed.

Thus it is,
O young Brahmin."

48. None in the crowd had heard anyone asking these questions. But as they with folded palms listened to the Master's answers, they were so filled with wonder and awe that they thought:

49. The people: "Who, indeed, has mentally posed these questions — a deity, Brahma, Indra or Sujampati? To whom did the Buddha respond?"

50. Ajita: "Bavari has asked about the head and its splitting. Explain this, O Sage, and remove this uncertainty."

51. *The Buddha: "Understand that the head*
Is Avijja (ignorance or error).
It is Vijja (knowledge or wisdom),
Along with faith, mindfulness,
Tranquillity and zealous exertion,
That splits or tears asunder
The head of ignorance."

52. Then with great gladness the Brahmin youth placed his cloak of deer skin on one shoulder, fell at the Buddha's feet and bowed his head.

53. Ajita: "The Brahmin Bavari and his jubilant disciples adore your feet respectfully and reverentially, O you with supernatural insight!"

54. *The Buddha: "May the Brahmin Bavari*
And his disciples
Have happiness!
Young Brahmin,
May you live long!"

55. "*Now you have the opportunity*
To ask any question
That you have in mind,

Whether it is about
Bavari's doubts,
Or those of yourself
Or anyone else."

56. After the Fully Awakened One granted permission, Ajita sat down with folded hands and then proceeded to pose the first question.

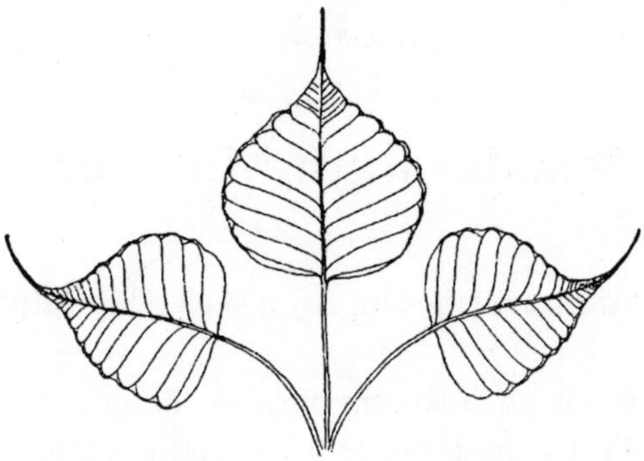

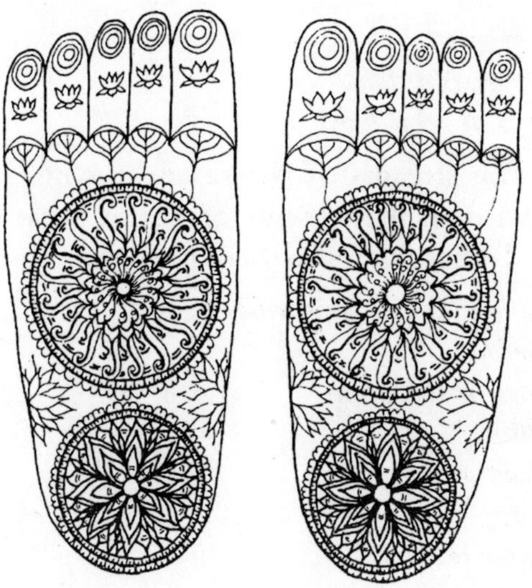

31

Wander forth Mindfully

In the **Ajitamanavapuccha** Ajita seeks the Buddha's advice.

1. Ajita: "What encloses the world? What prevents it from shining? What pollutes it? What is the world's great fear?"

2. *The Buddha: "Ignorance encloses the world.*
   It fails to shine
   Because of greed,
   Which, I say, is a stain.
   Suffering is its great fear."

3. Ajita: "The streams of desire are moving in all places. What can dam the streams of desire, what can restrain them and what can make them no longer flow?"

4. *The Buddha: "Whatever streams move*
   In the world,
   Mindfulness is the means
   To stop them.
   I talk about curbing them.
   Wisdom is
   A hindrance to them."

5. Ajita: "There is wisdom and, in addition, mindfulness.

Regarding name-and-form, O Venerable Sir, what will discontinue it?"

6. *The Buddha: "This question that you have posed,*
O Ajita, I will answer:
What brings about the end
Of name-and-form?
When there is
No consciousness
There is
No name-and-form either."

7. Ajita: "Regarding those who have weighed or estimated the Dharma, those under training and those ordinary persons here, O Venerable Sir, what mode of life do you recommend?"

8. *The Buddha: "Let the monk*
Not be greedy
For the pleasures of the senses.
Let him with
An unruffled mind
And with skilfulness in all Dhammas,
Wander forth mindfully."

32

Who is a Great Man?

In the **Tissametteyyamanavapuccha** Tissa Metteyya seeks the Buddha's advice.

1. Tissa Metteyya: "Who in this world is satisfied, who has no disturbances, and who, having seen the two extremes, remains intelligently unsullied by what is in between? Whom do you consider to be a great man? Who in the world has transcended desire?"

2. *The Buddha: "The monk*
Who leads a pure life
When surrounded by
Sensual pleasures,
Ever-aware,
Without craving,
Always attentive,
Who has attained tranquillity
By means of understanding,
It is he who is
Free from disturbances."

3. *"He who has seen*
The two extremes,

Remains unsullied
By what is in between,
Him do I consider to be
A great man,
For his craving
Has terminated."

In the above-mentioned verses "the two extremes" is probably a reference to the sense objects and the sense bases. The liberated state wherein there is no lurking attachment to the experiences arising from the interactions between the sense objects and the sense bases, is the most likely meaning of "remains unsullied by what is in between".

33

Going Beyond Birth and Old Age

In the **Punnakamanavapuccha** Punnaka seeks the Buddha's advice.

1. Punnaka: "I have come here to put a question to the Calm and Craving-Free One, who understands the roots. Why did the sages, warriors and Brahmins offer sacrifices to celestial beings here in this world? O Venerable One, I request you to tell me this."

2. *The Buddha: "These sages, warriors and Brahmins,*
   Beset by old age,
   Offered sacrifices to celestial beings
   In expectation of rebirth here."

3. Punnaka: "But did these sages, warriors and Brahmins, who ardently offered sacrifices to celestial beings, manage to transcend both birth and old age?"

4. *The Buddha: "They eagerly desired,*
   They praised,
   They prayed
   And they made sacrifices!
   They acted with the intention
   Of having sensual pleasures!

These sacrificers
With a passion
For future existence, I say,
Failed to transcend
Both birth and old age."

5. Punnaka: "If those devotees of sacrificial offerings did not succeed in going beyond birth and old age, then O Venerable One, who in the world of gods and men has gone beyond birth and old age?"

6. *The Buddha: "For him*
Who has taken into consideration
All and everything in the world,
O Punnaka,
There are no disturbances whatsoever.
He is calm,
Passionlessly devoid of fumes,
Free from suffering and desiring."

It is customary to light the sacred fire in many Brahmanical ceremonies of a sacrificial kind, whereas the Enlightened, as subtly alluded to in the last verse, are "passionlessly devoid of fumes" originating in the three ferocious fires of craving (*Lobha*), hatred (*Dosa*) and delusion (*Moha*).

34

In This Very Life

In the **Mettagumanavapuccha** Mettagu seeks the advice of the Buddha.

1. Mettagu: "I request you, O Venerable One, to tell me this, as I regard you as a perfect person with a thorough understanding of all conditions material and non-material. What is the source of the various forms of suffering in the world?"

2. *The Buddha: "You have asked me about*
The origin of suffering.
I will explain because I know it.
The many forms of suffering
In the world
Originate in
The substrata."

3. *"It is the ignorant man*
Who causes the substrata
To come into existence,
Thereby foolishly bringing on himself
Suffering again and again.
Therefore, seeing that suffering

Springs from the substrata,
The man of understanding
Ceases to create it."

4. Mettagu: "You have explained the question that we asked. Now we have another question that we request you to answer. How do the wise go beyond the stream of birth, old age, grief and mourning? Explain it fully, O Sage, for you have comprehended the Dharma."

5. *The Buddha: "I will expound to you,*
O Mettagu,
The Dharma,
Which has to be seen
By oneself directly
In this very life
Right here and now,
And which is not founded
On hearsay.

By understanding the Dharma,
And by wandering around mindfully
One can transcend
The attachments of this world."

6. Mettagu: "That supreme Dharma fills me with joy, O Great Sage (*Mahesi*), because by understanding the Dharma and by wandering around mindfully one can detach oneself from worldly enslavements."

7. *The Buddha: "Whatever you know,*
O Mettagu,
Be it below, above, across,
Or be it in between,
Do not take delight therein.
Do drop dogmas
And consciousness.

Then instead of stagnating
In existence
One goes beyond becoming."

8. *"Living likewise,*
Let the mindful and watchful monk,
After casting away
His self-centred attachments,
In this life itself
Give up birth, old age
And suffering."

9. Mettagu: "With great gladness I hear the Great Sage's well-expressed words about the state that is unstained by substrata. Surely you Venerable One have gone beyond suffering since you have discovered the Dharma."

10. "They are bound to get rid of suffering, whom you, O Sage, constantly instruct. Having come here to meet you, O Noble One, I bow before you. May the Venerable One constantly instruct me!"

11. *The Buddha: "The person*
Whom one can regard as
A knowledgeable
And genuine Brahmin

Not only owns nothing
But has also severed himself
From all sensuality.
Having crossed the stream,
He has moved to yonder shore.
He is free from mental obstructions
And devoid of doubt."

12. *"He is the wise one*
With the supreme knowledge.
No more has he any liking

For repeated existence.
His cravings ceased,
This desire-free person
No longer suffers.
I declare that
He has gone
Beyond birth and decay."

35

Crave Not for Repeated Existence

In the **Dhotakamanavapuccha** Dhotaka seeks the advice of the Buddha.

1. Dhotaka: "O Venerable One, please tell this to me. O Great Sage, I am eager to hear your words. After listening to you, I will train myself for my own liberation."

2. *The Buddha: "If that is so, be zealous!*
Here itself be prudent
And watchful!
Having listened to
What I shall tell you here,
Train yourself
For your own liberation!"

3. Dhotaka: "In the world of gods and men I can see in you the wandering Brahmin with no possessions whatsoever. So I bow before you in homage, O All-Seeing One (*Samantacakkhu*). O Sakyan, please cast off my uncertainties!"

4. *The Buddha: "I am not capable*
Of casting off
The uncertainties

Of anyone in the world,
O Dhotaka.
However, on understanding
The best Dharma
You will be able to cross
The stream."

5. Dhotaka: "Out of compassion for me, O Brahmin, teach me the Dharma of Detachment so that, like the open air that knows no suffering, I may live here in peace and freedom."

6. *The Buddha: "I will speak to you,*
O Dhotaka,
About the peace
That is not founded on hearsay,
Which when understood,
And when one has lived mindfully,

Enables one to transcend
All attachments in the world."

7. Dhotaka: "I approve of that supreme peace, O Great Sage, which when understood, and when one has lived mindfully, enables one to transcend all attachments in the world."

8. *The Buddha: "Whatever you know,*
O Dhotaka,
Be it below,
Above, across,
Or be it in between,
Seeing this
As a bond in the world,
Crave not
For repeated existence."

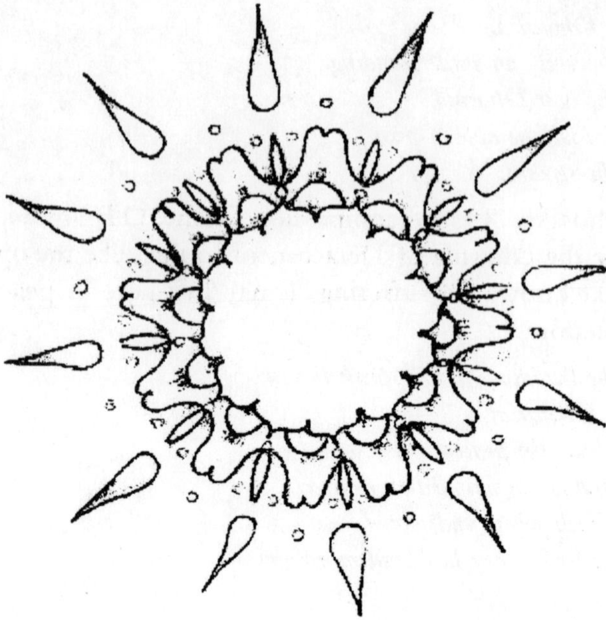

36

The State of Emancipation Defies Description

In the **Upasivamanavapuccha** Upasiva seeks the advice of the Buddha.

1. Upasiva: "All alone and without any help, O Sakyan, I will not be able to cross the great stream. O All-Seeing One, do tell me this. On what must I meditate, so that I can get beyond the stream?"

2. *The Buddha: "Observing the state*
   Of nothingness,
   Be attentive.
   Realising that
   Nothing exists,
   Do cross the stream.
   Discard the pleasures of the senses,
   Desist from doubting day and night,
   And you will see
   The ending of craving."

3. Upasiva: "The person whose passion for all sensual pleasures has died out, who is devoted to nothingness, after deserting all else, emancipation from perception being

the highest release, will he remain there without continuing as a samsaric migrant?"

4. *The Buddha: "When in a person*
The passion for all sensual pleasures
Has gone away,
When there is
Devotion to nothingness,
All else having disappeared,
Emancipation from perception
Being the highest release,
He will remain there
Without continuing
As a samsaric migrant."

5. Upasiva: "If he remains there free from samsaric servitude for a great many years, O All-Seeing One, and should he find Emancipation there, will his consciousness cease?"

6. *The Buddha: "As a flickering flame,*
Which blew out
In the wild wind
And disappeared for good,
Can no longer be regarded
As being a flame,
So a sage
Liberated from name-and-form
Cannot be called by any name
And cannot be defined."

7. Upasiva: "As regards the Liberated One, who has disappeared, does he not continue to exist? Is he affliction-free forever?"

8. *The Buddha: "There are no means*
Of measuring the man
Who has disappeared.
Nothing has he left behind

Whereby he can be described.
When all phenomena are gone,
Gone also are all means
Of description."

37

Going Across the Stream

In the **Nandamanavapuccha** Nanda seeks the Buddha's advice.

1. Nanda: "People speak about sages in the world. How do you view this matter? Do they say that a sage is one with knowledge or one who has a particular lifestyle?"

2. *The Buddha: "Not because of their views,*
Learning, knowledge
Nor because of tradition
Do the experts declare
That someone is a sage,
O Nanda.
I regard as sages only those
Who are disarming,
Free from suffering
And also free
From desire."

3. *Nanda:* "Ascetics and Brahmins state that purity is the outcome of views, tradition, virtue and good works, among many other things. O Venerable One, while leading lives

of restraint, did they manage to transcend birth and decay?
I request you to tell me this."

4. *The Buddha: "Ascetics and Brahmins,*
O Nanda,
State that purity
Is the outcome
Of views, tradition,
Virtue and good works,
Among many other things.
Although they lived restrainedly,
I can tell you
That none of them succeeded
In going beyond
Birth and decay."

5. Nanda: "Ascetics and Brahmins state that purity is the outcome of views, tradition, virtue and good works, among many other things. You say, O Sage, that none of them succeeded in going beyond birth and decay. In that case, O Venerable One, who in the world of gods and men succeeded in doing that? Do please explain this to me."

6. *The Buddha: "I am not saying,*
O Nanda,
That all ascetics and Brahmins
Are subject to birth and decay.
There are those
Who let go
Of all that was seen,
Heard or thought,
Who put a stop
To ascetic practices
And vows,
Who dropped
Everything of different kinds,

And finally ceased
To crave.
They did indeed
Cross the stream."

7. Nanda: "I rejoice at the well-spoken words of the Great Rishi (*Mahesi*) Gotama, which are without acquisitions (*Upadhi*).

Those persons in this place who have discarded all that was seen, heard or thought, who have put a stop to ascetic practices and vows, who have dropped everything of different kinds and have also ceased to crave, they, too, I say, have gone across the stream."

38

Serenity Here and Now

In the **Hemakamanavapuccha** Hemaka seeks the Buddha's advice.

1. Hemaka: "Before coming across the teachings of Gotama, what I had heard previously — 'so it was, so it will be' — were only hearsay-based beliefs, which made me more doubtful."

1. "I was not delighted by that, but teach me the Dharma that results in the rooting out of craving, which, O Sage, enables a mindful man to cease clinging in the world."

3. *The Buddha: "The dropping*
Of all attachment
To whatever is deemed
Dear in the world
Anything that has been seen,
Heard, thought
Or experienced,
O Hemaka,
Is the everlasting
State of Nirvana."

4. *"Understanding this,*

The mindful
Who have attained Serenity
In this very birth,
Are always tranquil
And they in this world
Have transcended desire."

39

What is the Nature of Emancipation?

In the **Todeyyamanavapuccha** Todeyya seeks the Buddha's advice.

1. Todeyya: "What sort of Emancipation is there for the person who has dropped sensuality, cravings and doubts?"

2. *The Buddha: "As regards the person*
Who has dropped sensuality,
Cravings and doubts,
For him there is
No other Emancipation."

3. Todeyya: "Is such a person free from desire or still yearning? Has he realised wisdom or is he trying to acquire it? O Sakyan, the All-Seeing One, please clarify this, so that I would be able to notice a sage."

4. *The Buddha: "Not only is the sage*
Devoid of desire
But also
No longer yearning.
Not only has he
Realised wisdom
But he also

Does not have to acquire it.
You can,
O Todeyya,
By this means
Recognise the sage,
For he owns nothing,
And is not at all attached
To sensual pleasures
And samsaric existence."

40

The Incomparable Island

In the **Kappamanavapuccha** Kappa seeks the Buddha's advice.

1. Kappa: "For those left behind in the midst of the lake when the frightening flood waters surge, for those suffering from decay and death and wishing to surmount them, is there an island, O Sir, wherein these sufferings will never again come back?"

2. *The Buddha: "For those stranded*
In the midst of the lake
When the frightening
Flood waters surge,
For those suffering
From decay and death
And wishing to surmount them,
O Kappa,
I will tell you
Of an island."

3. *"This incomparable island*
Wherein there is neither
Decay nor death,

Which I name as Nirvana,
Is no other than
Owning nothing
And wanting nothing."

4. *"Those persons*
Who have perceived this
Are mindful.
As regards the world of sensation,
They are of cooled mind.
They are not obedient
To Mara.
They are not
Mara's slaves."

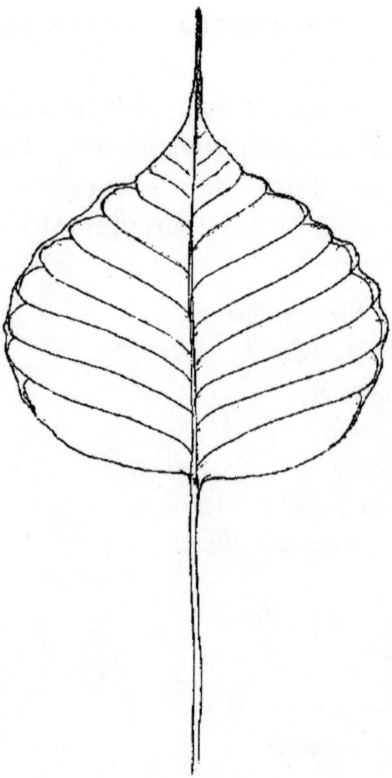

41

The Tranquil State

In the **Jatukannimanavapuccha** Jatukanni seeks the Buddha's advice.

1 Jatukanni: "After hearing about the hero, who has done away with all sensual pleasures and crossed the stream, I have come to ask about the tranquil state. O Venerable One, do speak about its nature."

2. "As on earth the sun's radiance stands out, so is the Venerable One, for he moves about after having surrendered sensuality. Great and profound is your wisdom but limited is my understanding! Please point out to me the Dharma, so that I can learn about the giving up of birth and decay here itself."

3. *The Buddha: "Put away the greed*
For sensual pleasures.
Regard the emancipation
From human passion
As a sure refuge.
Let there not remain
Within you anything
That you have either acquired

Or discarded."

4. *"May your past perish,*
May nothing flow forth
In the future.
In the intervening period
Do cease clinging.
Thereby you can traverse
The territory
With tranquility."

5. *"The person who is fully free*
From greed for name and form,
O Brahmin,
Has no Asavas (biases)
Whereby he would fall
Into the clutches of Mara."

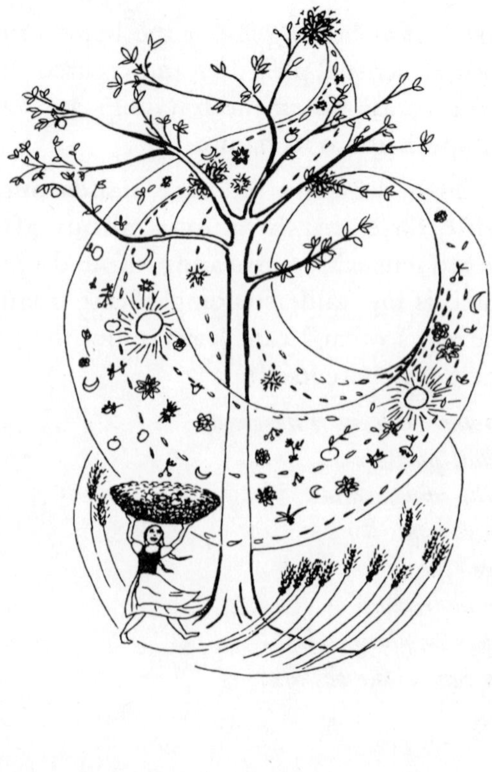

42

Why be Given to Grasping?

In the **Bhadravudhamanavapuccha** Bhadravudha seeks the Buddha's advice.

1. Bhadravudha: "I make an earnest request from the one who has abandoned every resting-place, who has cut down craving, who is free from lust, who has given up joy; who having overcome the flood, is released; who has left behind time and is very wise. After listening to the Buddha (*Naga*) they will leave this world."

   The phrase "the one who has abandoned every resting-place" might not necessarily refer to the homelessness entailed in the ascetic way of life of the monk. The giving up of "every resting-place" could, metaphorically speaking, refer as well to the emancipated mind that is without any settled views, ideas or beliefs. In other words, the perfect openness of the liberated mind is such that it never operates from any standpoint nor does it get stuck in dogmas, doctrines, theories and the like. Not taking up a position whatsoever on any subject or situation means not having any attitude towards it and also not having any opinion on it.

2. "Filled with longing for your words, O Hero (*Vira*), various people from the country have assembled. Please explain to them the Dharma that you have realised."

3. *The Buddha: "Keep away from all craving,*
O Bhadravudha,
Be it below,
Above, across,
Or be it in between.
Because anything
They hang onto
In the world,
Mara will use that
To follow them."

4. *"Therefore, the monk*
Who understands this,
Being mindful,
Never takes hold
Of anything
In the whole world.
Observe that all living beings
Are given to grasping,
Hence they are in the realm
Of Mara,
Which is the sphere
Of death."

43

Rejoice Not in Sensations

In the **Udayamanavapuccha** Udaya seeks the Buddha's advice.

1. Udaya: "I have come with a question to the seated meditator, who has attained meditative absorption (*Jhana*) and is devoid of defilements, who has fulfilled his obligations, this perfect person who has gone to the shore beyond. Tell me of deliverance by means of the highest insight and the breaking up of ignorance."

2. *The Buddha: "Rid yourself of sensuous desire,*
   O Udaya,
   As well as melancholy.
   Let go of laziness
   And bad behaviour."

3. *"I talk about deliverance*
   By means of
   The highest insight
   And the breaking up
   Of ignorance.
   There is right reasoning,
   And then there is

The purity
That is the outcome
Of equanimity,
Which is the neutral
Evenness of mind."

4. Udaya: "What in the world binds us to continued existence? What is it like? By the leaving behind of what is Nirvana attained?"

5. *The Buddha: "The world is in the bondage*
Of rejoicing.
Reflecting on it
Is its investigation.
The giving up of craving
Is called Nirvana."

6. Udaya: "How does consciousness cease when one is mindful? Having come to the Venerable One we like to hear your advice."

7. *The Buddha: "When a man is mindful*
And does not rejoice
In sensations,
Regardless of whether
His sensations arise within
And are personal and subjective,
Or whether
His sensations arise outside
And are impersonal and objective,
Then only does consciousness cease."

44

Nothing Either Inside or Outside

In the **Posalamanavapuccha** Posala seeks the Buddha's advice.

1. Posala: "To the one who shows the past, who is devoid of both desire and doubt and who has transcended all phenomena, I have come with the intention of posing a question."

2. "I ask you, O Sakyan, about the knowledge of the one who has gone beyond the perception of forms, who has renounced all corporeality and who also sees that there is nothing either inside or outside. Can such a person be led to a greater extent?"

3. *The Buddha: "The Tathagata (the Perfect One)*
Knows all the stations
Of consciousness,
O Posala,
He knows the one
Who is released
As well as the one
Devoted to Emancipation."

4. *"Having discovered*

The state of nothingness,
He regards rejoicing
As nothing
But a bond.
Seeing this to be so,
He obtains an insight into it.
This is the true knowledge
Of the perfect Brahmin."

Meditation involves the passive, impartial, neutral and non-judgemental observation of one's thoughts, feelings and sensations, doing so as these arise, as these stay for awhile and then as these slip away. In the **Dhyana Mudra** the hands are relaxed in the lap, the right hand is placed over the left, the palms face upwards and the two thumbs touch at their tips.

45

Be Mindful Always

In the **Mogharajamanavapuccha** Mogharaja seeks the Buddha's advice.

1. Mogharaja: "On two separate occasions, O Sakyan, I have asked a question but the All-Wise-Seer (*Cakkhuma*) did not give an answer. I have heard that celestial seers answer questions only when asked the third time."

2. "I do not know how the renowned Gotama regards this world, the next world and the Brahma world with its celestial beings."

3. "I have come to put a question to the one with such excellent insight. How must one perceive the world so as not to be observed by the King of Death (*Maccuraja*)?"

4. *The Buddha: "Mogharaja,*
Be mindful always.
By looking at
The emptiness
Or the void
That characterises the world,
And by dropping the view that
The 'self' exists,

One defeats death.
The King of Death
Will fail to observe the person
Who perceives the world
In the aforementioned manner."

46

Be Finished with Forms

In the **Pingiyamanavapuccha** Pingiya seeks the Buddha's advice.

1. Pingiya: "I am aged, weak and colourless; my eyes cannot see clearly and my hearing is impaired. So that I do not perish while still being stupid, show me the Dharma that might enable me to overcome the process of birth and decay in this present life."

2. *The Buddha: "Seeing how living beings*
   Suffer because of forms —
   The heedless are hurt
   Because of forms —
   Be alert, Pingiya,
   And do give up forms
   So that renewed existence
   Comes to an end."

3. Pingiya: "In the ten regions — the four regions, the four intermediate regions, above and below — there is nothing in the world that has not been seen, heard, thought or understood by you. Show me the Dharma so that the process of birth and decay comes to a stop here."

4. *The Buddha: "Observing how creatures*
Controlled by craving,
O Pingiya,
Are tormented
And destroyed
By old age,
Be mindful and devoid
Of Tanha (desire or thirst),
So that you may
Never again
Come into existence."

47

The Path to Yonder Shore

The final section of the Sutta-Nipata, which is called the **Parayanasutta**, is full of Pingiya's praise for the extraordinarily great personal qualities of the Buddha as well as the profound Dharma. His devotion to the Teacher and his message inspires Pingiya with enthusiasm for Enlightenment.

Thus spoke the Venerable One when he was living in Magadha at the Rock Shrine called Pasanaka. There he answered each of the questions posed by the sixteen Brahmins, who were followers of Bavari. If any person fully understands the meaning of any one of these questions, and lives in accordance with the Dharma thereafter, he will go to the Further Shore. For this reason this particular exposition of the teachings is called "Going to the Beyond".

1. Ajita, Tissametteyya, Punnaka, Mettagu, Dhotaka, Upasiva, Nanda and Hemaka,
2. Todeyya, Kappa, Jatukani the pundit, Bhadravudha, Udaya, Posala, Mogharaja the wise and Pingiya the holy man —
3. These persons approached the Buddha, the Sage who leads the perfect moral life. They visited the best Buddha, asking abstruse questions.

4. When he was questioned, the Buddha expounded the Truth as it really is. His answers made the Brahmins happy.
5. Having been made happy by the All-Wise-Seer (Cakkhuma), the Kinsman of the Sun (Adiccabandhu), they led lives of purity near the One of Supreme Wisdom (Varapanno).
6. Should anyone walk the way as shown by the Buddha in his answer to any single question, he shall proceed from this shore to the Shore Beyond.
7. One would proceed from this shore to the Shore Beyond, provided one has developed along the highest path. This path is for crossing over to the Shore Beyond. Therefore it is termed "the path to the Shore Beyond".

   Pingiya returned to the Godhavari and informed Bavari about everything that had happened.

8. *Pingiya: "Through song I will tell you*
   Of the way to the Shore Beyond.
   He stated it as he saw it.
   He is spotless and very intelligent.
   He is the lust-free Lord.
   Why should he speak falsely?"
9. *"Well! I will praise the voice*
   Of him who gave up
   The stain of delusion,
   And let go of pride
   And hypocrisy."
10. *"The Buddha, the dispeller of darkness,*
    The All-Seeing One (Samantacakkhu),
    Who fully comprehends the world,
    Who overcame becoming,
    Who is free from cankers,
    Who left behind all suffering,
    And who is true to his name,

Him do I serve, O Brahmin."

11. *"As a bird that has left a brushwood*
With small trees and shrubs,
Wishing instead to live
In a forest with many fruits,
So have I left those with little wisdom
And found him,
Just like a swan
That finds the great ocean."

12. *"Those in another world,*
Before the Dispensation of Gotama,
Declared 'thus it was, thus it will be'.
That was mere oral tradition,
Which tended to increase doubts."

13. *"Unique dispeller of darkness,*
Seated, high-born,
This Light-Bringer (Pabhankaro),
Gotama the One of Great Wisdom (Bhuripannano),
Gotama the Very Intelligent One (Bhurimedhaso),"

14. *"Who showed me the Dharma*
That is actual and timeless,
The ending of craving
And the detachment from distress,
The likeness of which
Cannot be found anywhere."

15. Bavari: "How can you, O Pingiya, absent yourself even for a second from Gotama the One of Great Wisdom, from Gotama the Very Intelligent One,"

16. "Who showed you the Dharma that is actual and timeless, the ending of craving and the detachment from distress, the likeness of which cannot be found anywhere?"

17. *Pingiya: "O Brahmin, I cannot*

Absent myself even for a second
From Gotama the One of Great Wisdom,
From Gotama the Very Intelligent One,"

18. *"Who showed me the Dharma*
That is actual and timeless,
The ending of craving
And the detachment from distress,
The likeness of which
Cannot be found anywhere."

19. *"I know him with my mind*
As with my eye the day and night.
O Brahmin, being vigilant, I spend
The night honouring him.
On account of that itself
I consider that there is
No absentmindedness."

20. *"My faith and joy and mindfulness*
Bend towards the message of Gotama.
Towards wherever the One
Of Great Wisdom walks,
Thereto I am bent."

21. *"I am broken up*
And my strength is failing,
And because of that
The body cannot flee there,
Yet with watchful thought
I constantly go there,
For my mind, O Brahmin,
Is connected to him."

22. *"While lying in the mud*
Of moral impurity,
With my wavering mind
I swam from one resting-place

To another resting-place!
Then I saw the Perfectly Enlightened
Or Universal Buddha (Sammasambuddha),
Who has surmounted
The flood of ignorance and desire
And who is taintless (Anasavam)."

The Buddha appears on the scene either in person or in a mysterious way that is difficult to explain.

23. *The Buddha: "Just as Vakkali,*
Who was given to faith
And found release,
And Bhadravudha
Along with Alavi-Gotama,
In the same way
May you be freed
Through faith
And may you, Pingiya,
Proceed beyond
The realm of death."

24. *Pingiya: "I am all the more devoted here*
On hearing the words of the Sage,
The Perfectly Enlightened One.
He who has uncovered the veil
Is open-hearted and quick-witted."

25. *"Knowing all that is superior to the gods,*
He discovered both
The heavenly sphere
And the earthly one.
The Teacher put an end
To the questions of the uncertain
Who did recognise the truth."

26. *"Certainly I will go*
To the Immovable (Asanhira = Nirvana),

The Unshakable (Asankuppa = Nirvana),
Which is beyond compare anywhere.
In this matter I have no doubt.
Regard my mind as being thus inclined."

Bibliography

Burlingame, Eugene Watson *Buddhist Legends*, translated from the original Pali text of the Dhammapada Commentary. Oxford: Pali Text Society, 1995

Chalmers, Sir Robert *Buddha's Teachings, being the Sutta-Nipata or Discourse Collection*, edited in the original Pali text with an English version facing it. Delhi : Motilal Banarsidass, 1997

Childers, Robert Caesar *A Dictionary of the Pali Language*. London: Trubner, 1875

Fausboll, V *The Sutta Nipata : a Collection of Discourses* 2nd ed. revised translated from the Pali (The Sacred Books of the East, 10) Delhi : Motilal Banarsidass, 1980

Hare, E.M *Woven Cadences of Early Buddhists*, translated from the Pali (The Sacred Books of the Buddhists, 15) London: Geoffrey Cumberlege, 1947

Ireland, John D *The Discourse Collection: Selected Texts from the Sutta Nipata*, translated from the Pali Kandy : Buddhist Publication Society, 1965

Jayawickrama, N. A *Suttanipata*, Pali text with translation into English and notes Kelaniya (Sri Lanka) Post-Graduate Institute of Pali & Buddhist Studies, University of Kelaniya, 2001

Malalasekera, *G.P Dictionary of Pali Proper Names* New Delhi : Munshiram Manoharlal, 1983

Narada (Maha Thera) *The Buddha and His Teachings* Colombo : Vajirarama, 1973

Norman, K.R *The Group of Discourses (Sutta-Nipata)*, vol. 2 revised translation with introduction and notes Oxford: Pali Text Society, 1995

Nyanatiloka (the Venerable) *Buddhist Dictionary: Manual of Buddhist Terms and Doctrines*, 3rd revised and enlarged edition, edited by Nyanaponika Taipei: Corporate Body of the Buddha Educational Foundation,circa 1987

Rhys Davids, T.W *Pali-English Dictionary*, edited by T. W. Rhys Davids and William Stede New Delhi: Munshiram Manoharlal, 2001